Y0-AQR-775

Especially for
From
Date

Print ISBN 978-1-62836-647-1

eBook Editions:
Adobe Digital Edition (.epub) 978-1-63058-083-4
Kindle and MobiPocket Edition (.prc) 978-1-63058-084-1

Published by Barbour Publishing, Inc., P.O. Box 719, Uhrichsville, Ohio 44683, www.barbourbooks.com

Our mission is to publish and distribute inspirational products offering exceptional value and biblical encouragement to the masses.

Printed in China.

Daily Whispers of Blessing

Look Forward

Instead of feeling sorry for ourselves as we advance in years, or toting up the days and months that are already past, let's praise God for all the benefits He's already given and look forward to all those that may lie ahead.

His Perfect Plan

Every experience God gives us, every person He puts in our lives, is the perfect preparation for the future that only He can see.

—CORRIE TEN BOOM

The Best Things

The best things are nearest: breath in your nostrils, light in your eyes, flowers at your feet, duties at your hand, the path of Right just before you. Do not grasp at the stars, but do life's plain common work as it comes, certain that daily duties and daily bread are the sweetest things in life.

—ROBERT LOUIS STEVENSON

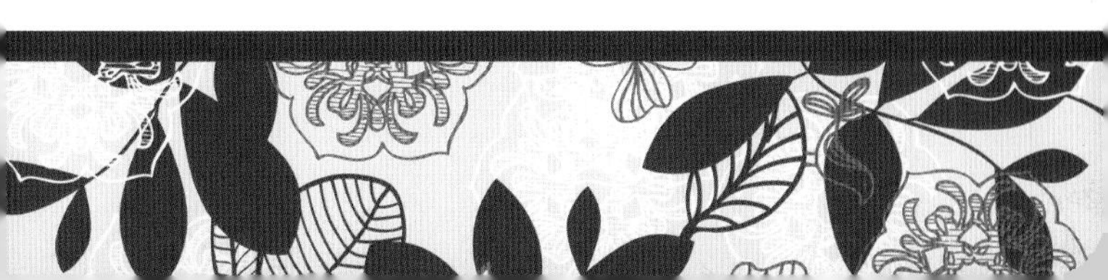

Spiritual Blessings

Let us honor and thank the God and
Father of our Lord Jesus Christ. He has already
given us a taste of what heaven is like.

—EPHESIANS 1:3 NLV

Unbelievable Faith

In the present state of things, [faith] is the only means under heaven for establishing the law of love. On that account, it is an unspeakable blessing to us.

Beautiful Dawn

How beautiful it is to be alive!
To wake each morning as if the Maker's
grace did us afresh from nothingness derive,
that we might sing, "How happy is our case!
How beautiful it is to be alive!"

—HENRY SEPTIMUS SUTTON

He Longs to Listen

Isn't it great that God wants us to talk to Him about all of our worries and cares? What a gift that He cares about everything that happens to us every step of the way.

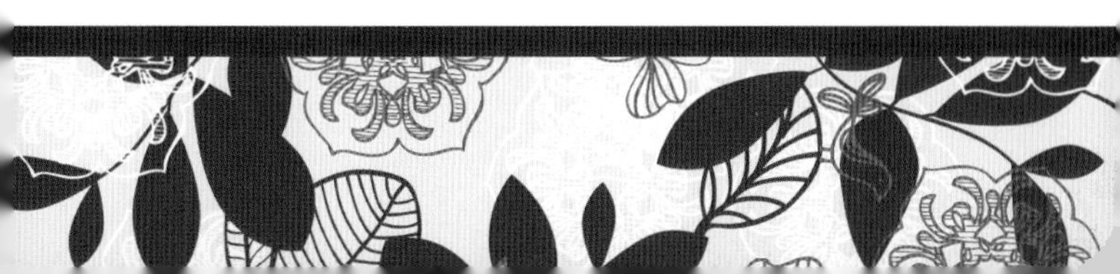

The Best Is Yet to Come

Our heavenly Father never takes anything from His children unless He means to give them something better.

—GEORGE MACDONALD

How Refreshing!

The beauty and loveliness of all things
are fading and perishing, but the loveliness
of Christ is fresh for all eternity.

Divine Providence

You will eat the fruit of your labor;
blessings and prosperity will be yours. Your wife
will be like a fruitful vine within your house;
your sons will be like olive shoots around your
table. Thus is the man blessed
who fears the LORD.

—PSALM 128:2–4 NIV

Eternal Gratitude

Lord, thank You for every blessing,
both big and small. Help me to be more aware
of the ways in which You take care of me,
so my gratitude can continue to grow. Amen.

DAY 12

Be Prepared

Above all else, know this: Be prepared at all times for the gifts of God and be ready always for new ones. For God is a thousand times more ready to give than we are to receive.

—MEISTER ECKHART

Wonderful Plans

God is still in control of every situation. The universe belongs to Him, including all the people in it. At such a time as this, He may be planning something wonderful a mere step beyond the problem we face. Just because we don't see the blessing yet doesn't mean it isn't on its way.

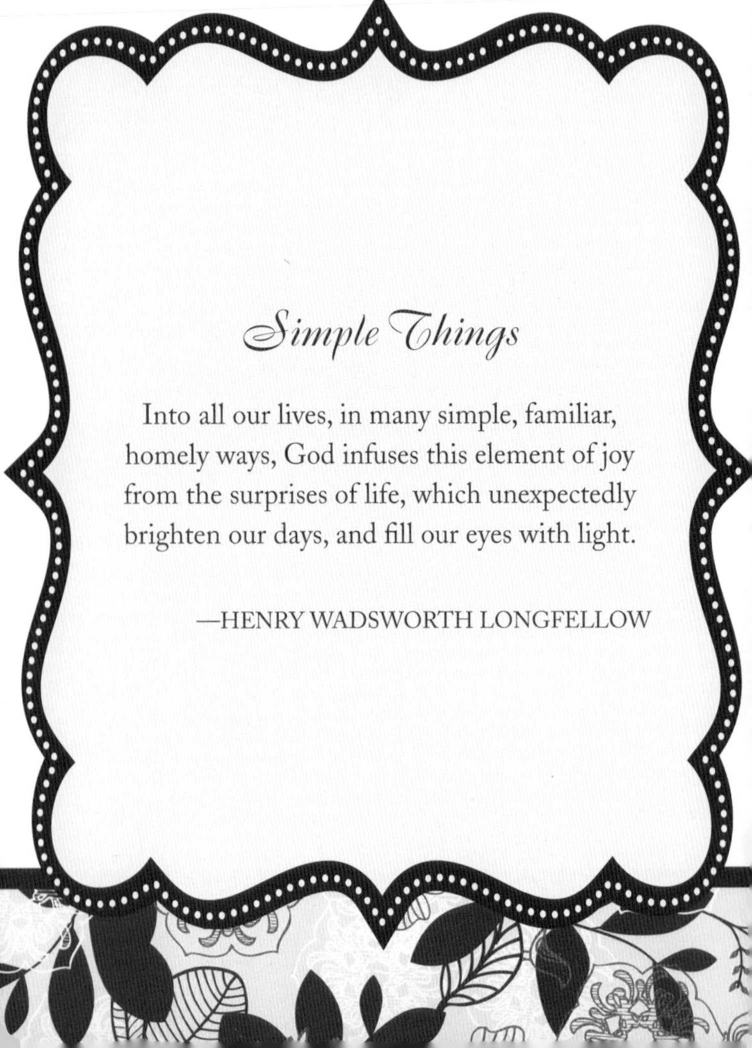

Simple Things

Into all our lives, in many simple, familiar, homely ways, God infuses this element of joy from the surprises of life, which unexpectedly brighten our days, and fill our eyes with light.

—HENRY WADSWORTH LONGFELLOW

Heart Gifts

It's not the things that can be bought
That are life's richest treasures,
It's just the little gifts from the heart
That money cannot measure.
A cheerful smile, a friendly word,
A sympathetic nod,
All priceless little treasures
From the storehouse of our God.

—HELEN STEINER RICE

Blessings Always

"I will make you into a great nation and I will bless you; I will make your name great, and you will be a blessing. I will bless those who bless you, and whoever curses you I will curse; and all peoples on earth will be blessed through you."

—GENESIS 12:2–3 NIV

Instant Comfort

Faith is the root of all blessings. Believe and you shall be saved; believe and you must needs be satisfied; believe and you cannot but be comforted.

—JEREMY TAYLOR

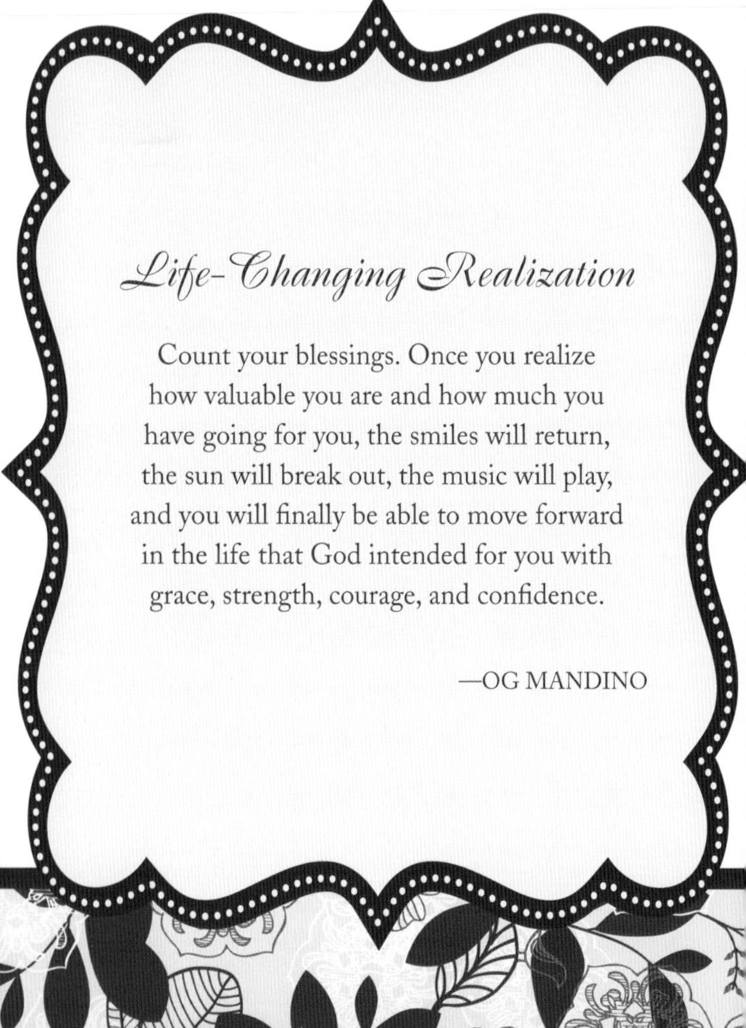

Life-Changing Realization

Count your blessings. Once you realize how valuable you are and how much you have going for you, the smiles will return, the sun will break out, the music will play, and you will finally be able to move forward in the life that God intended for you with grace, strength, courage, and confidence.

—OG MANDINO

The Cycle of Joy

When we've made it our lifestyle to take hold of God's Word and teachings and use them to show others how to live, we are truly blessed—and so are others who come in contact with us. Their growth in turn touches others' lives—and on and on it goes. The joys of mercy, peace, and love abound, just as God planned.

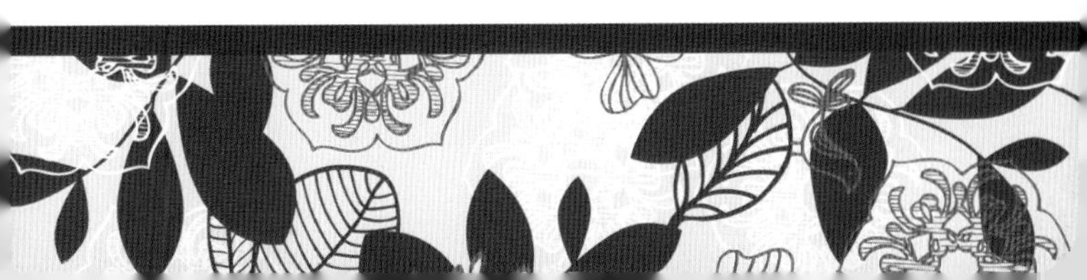

Open Your Eyes

I have always thought it would be a blessing
if each person could be blind and deaf for a
few days during his early adult life.
Darkness would make him appreciate sight;
silence would teach him the joys of sound.

—HELEN KELLER

Hidden Blessings

God left the world unfinished;
the pictures unpainted, the songs unsung,
and the problems unsolved, that man
might know the joys of creation.

—THOMAS S. MONSON

Giving

"Give, and it will be given to you. A good measure, pressed down, shaken together and running over, will be poured into your lap. For with the measure you use, it will be measured to you."

—LUKE 6:38 NIV

Seek His Guidance

Lord, You've given me a life that abounds in rich blessings, and You've guaranteed that because of this, You also have great expectations of me. Help me to be faithful to these expectations. Amen.

Seasonal Blessings

The four seasons. . .demonstrate creation's thankfulness to God for a job well done. The trees bow before heaven as their leaves fall gracefully to the ground. The glistening snowfall speaks of God's majesty. Flowers of every kind bow low to the glory of God in spring, and summer warms to the glow of all the blessings God has to offer.

Only One

Most of all other beautiful things in life come by twos and threes, by dozens and hundreds. Plenty of roses, stars, sunsets, rainbows, brothers and sisters, aunts and cousins, but only one mother in the whole world.

—KATE DOUGLAS WIGGIN

Bearable Burdens

Lord, we sometimes sing a song about being happy because You took our burdens all away. I guess You really just made the burdens more bearable. Still, that's something great to sing about, and it does bring happiness. I'm so glad You're there to lighten the load.

Enjoy Being Alive

Life is what we are alive to. It is not length but breadth. . . . Be alive. . .to goodness, kindness, purity, love, history, poetry, music, flowers, stars, God, and eternal hope.

—MALTBIE D. BABCOCK

Sweet Assurance

My blessings are so many, my troubles are so few
How can I be discouraged when
I know that I have You?
And I have the sweet assurance that
there's nothing I need fear
If I but keep remembering
I am Yours and You are near,
For anything and everything can
somehow be endured
If Your presence is beside me and lovingly assured.

—HELEN STEINER RICE

Present Reflection

Reflect upon your present blessings,
of which every man has many, not of your past
misfortunes, of which all men have some.

—CHARLES DICKENS

Proof We Can Rely On

At the end of each month, I read over my prayer journal and see where God has done miraculous things. . . . If I can list a number of answers to specific prayers in January, I feel better prepared to trust God in February.

—BILL HYBELS

God's Faithfulness

God has blessed us with a relationship with
Himself. He is faithful to us, too.
Despite our mistakes,
God still loves us and gives us great blessings. . . .
Let us believe God and walk faithfully in
His way through all our days.

With Worship and Honor

Thanks be to You, Jesus Christ, for the many
gifts Thou hast bestowed on me. . . .
I am giving Thee worship with my whole life. . . .
I am giving Thee honour with my whole utterance.

—CARMINA GADELICA

Indulge

Don't put off for tomorrow what you can do today, because if you enjoy it today, you can do it again tomorrow.

—JAMES A. MICHENER

Rejoice!

This is the day that the Lord has made;
let us rejoice and be glad in it. . . . Blessed is he
who comes in the name of the Lord! We bless
you from the house of the Lord. The Lord is
God, and he has made his light to shine upon
us. . . . You are my God, and I will give thanks
to you; you are my God; I will extol you.

—PSALM 118:24, 26–28 ESV

Awesome Generosity

What a wonderful, giving God we serve. He stands with extended hand, ready to give you the desires of your heart. Take a moment to offer thanks to Him for the greatest gifts, the awesome joys you've experienced, and even the small things that you realize He engineered to bless you in an unexpected way.

Bless God

If you can eat today, enjoy the sunlight today,
mix good cheer with friends today,
enjoy it and bless God for it.

—HENRY WARD BEECHER

Enjoying Good Health

I thank You, Father, for giving me good health. There are so many who do not enjoy this blessing. Sometimes I'm tempted to complain about the aches and pains we all face from time to time, but I really have no reason to. You have been good to me.

A Spiritual Scent

God's holy beauty comes near you like a spiritual scent, and it stirs your drowsing soul. . . . He creates in you the desire to find Him and run after Him—to follow wherever He leads you, and to press peacefully against His heart wherever He is.

—JOHN OF THE CROSS

The Power of Love

Love is a great thing, an altogether good gift, the only thing that makes burdens light and bears all that is hard with ease. It carries a weight without feeling it and makes all that is bitter sweet and pleasant to the taste.

—THOMAS À KEMPIS

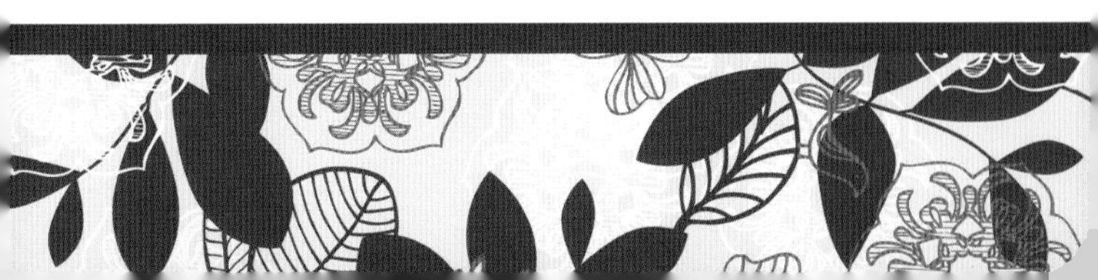

Let Your Admiration Show

When I look at your heavens, the work of your
fingers, the moon and the stars, which you have
set in place, what is man that you are mindful of
him, and the son of man that you care for him?
Yet you have made him a little lower than the
heavenly beings and crowned him
with glory and honor.

—PSALM 8:3–5 ESV

A Guidepost for Prayer

Our prayers should be for blessings in general,
for God knows best what is good for us.

—SOCRATES

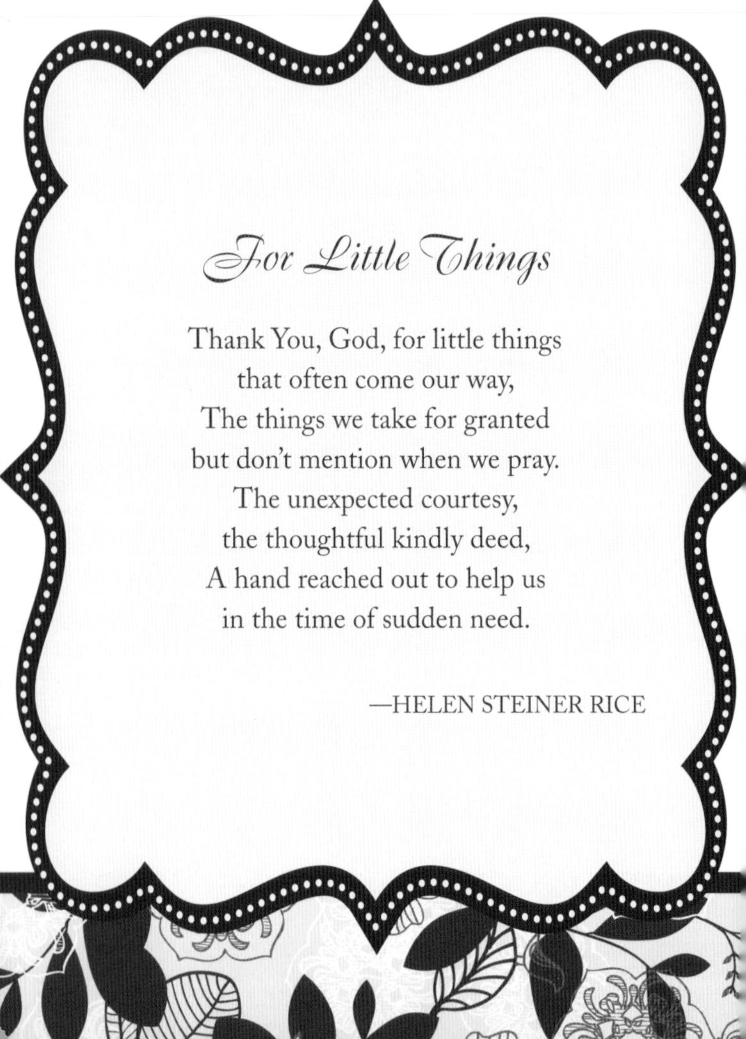

For Little Things

Thank You, God, for little things
that often come our way,
The things we take for granted
but don't mention when we pray.
The unexpected courtesy,
the thoughtful kindly deed,
A hand reached out to help us
in the time of sudden need.

—HELEN STEINER RICE

Restored Living

We all know what it feels like to be at rest. . . .
But are we willing to leave the press long enough
to lie down in the soothing green pastures and to
be led by the still waters of His provision?

—PATSY CLAIRMONT

Blessed Friends

Nothing opens the heart like another person
with whom you may share all your
hopes, fears, and joys.

—UNKNOWN

Open Up!

He is always willing to relieve our needs. The chief thing lacking is a suitable disposition on our part to receive His grace and blessing.

Wholly His

How blessed is God! And what a blessing
he is! He's the Father of our Master,
Jesus Christ, and takes us to the high places
of blessing in him. Long before he laid down
earth's foundations, he had us in mind,
had settled on us as the focus of his love,
to be made whole and holy by his love.

—EPHESIANS 1:3–4 MSG

Making a Connection

The joy of receiving is far more than the gifts—
that when we receive graciously and gladly,
we reciprocate the gift with joy and gratitude;
and in that moment of shared happiness and
understanding, giver and receiver "connect."

—JENNY WALTON

The Art of Life

The art of life is to live in the present moment and to make that moment as perfect as we can by the realization that we are the instruments and expression of God Himself.

—EMMET FOX

Peacemakers, Rejoice!

God blesses our efforts for peace, though they may not bear fruit immediately. We draw closer to God, even if we cannot improve the lives of others. God doesn't command that we will be successful in our peacemaking, though we may be. He only requires us to work at it. Blessings for that obedience will still come from His hand.

Blessed Solitude

I feel the same way about solitude as some people feel about the blessing of the church. It's the light of grace for me. I never close my door behind me without the awareness that I am carrying out an act of mercy toward myself.

—PETER HOEG

Full-Circle Blessings

If you affirm goodness, goodness will be there;
if you affirm love, love will be there;
if you affirm thankfulness, blessings will come.
A good place to begin is by giving praise
and thanks to Almighty God.

—NORMAN VINCENT PEALE

Stop Chasing

I say it is better to be content with what little you have. Otherwise, you will always be struggling for more, and that is like chasing the wind.

—ECCLESIASTES 4:6 NCV

Generations of Thanks

God help us to be grateful for our blessings, never to be guilty of the sin of ingratitude, and to instill this same gratitude into the lives of our children.

—EZRA TAFT BENSON

Wayside Sacraments

Never lose an opportunity of seeing
anything that is beautiful; for beauty is
God's handwriting—a wayside sacrament.
Welcome it in every fair face, in every fair sky,
in every fair flower, and thank God
for it as a cup of blessing.

—RALPH WALDO EMERSON

No More Distractions

When we put aside the things that would distract us from God, our lives are fully blessed. We can worship Him for the things He has given us—the physical and spiritual joys that leap off our tongues as we think of all our Savior has given.

Discover Life's Blessings

As we grow in our capacities to discover the joys that God has placed in our lives, life becomes a glorious experience of discovering His endless wonders.

Priceless Gifts

This brings you a million good wishes and more
For the things you cannot buy in a store:
Faith to sustain you in times of trial,
A joy-filled heart and a happy smile,
Contentment, inner peace, and love—
All priceless gifts from God above!

—HELEN STEINER RICE

Generous Hearts

The world of the generous gets larger
and larger. . . . The one who blesses
others is abundantly blessed;
those who help others are helped.

—PROVERBS 11:24–25 MSG

Rekindled Awareness

In everyone's life, at some time, our inner fire goes out. It is then burst into flame by an encounter with another human being. We should all be thankful for those people who rekindle the inner spirit.

—ALBERT SCHWEITZER

Glorious Day

It is the first mild day of March: each minute sweeter than before. . . . There is a blessing in the air, which seems a sense of joy to yield.

—WILLIAM WORDSWORTH

Satisfied!

Continue to walk steadily with your Lord, and He'll fulfill many more desires. Then, at the end of life, you'll see that any He left behind were best done so, and you'll offer this one-word testimony: Satisfied!

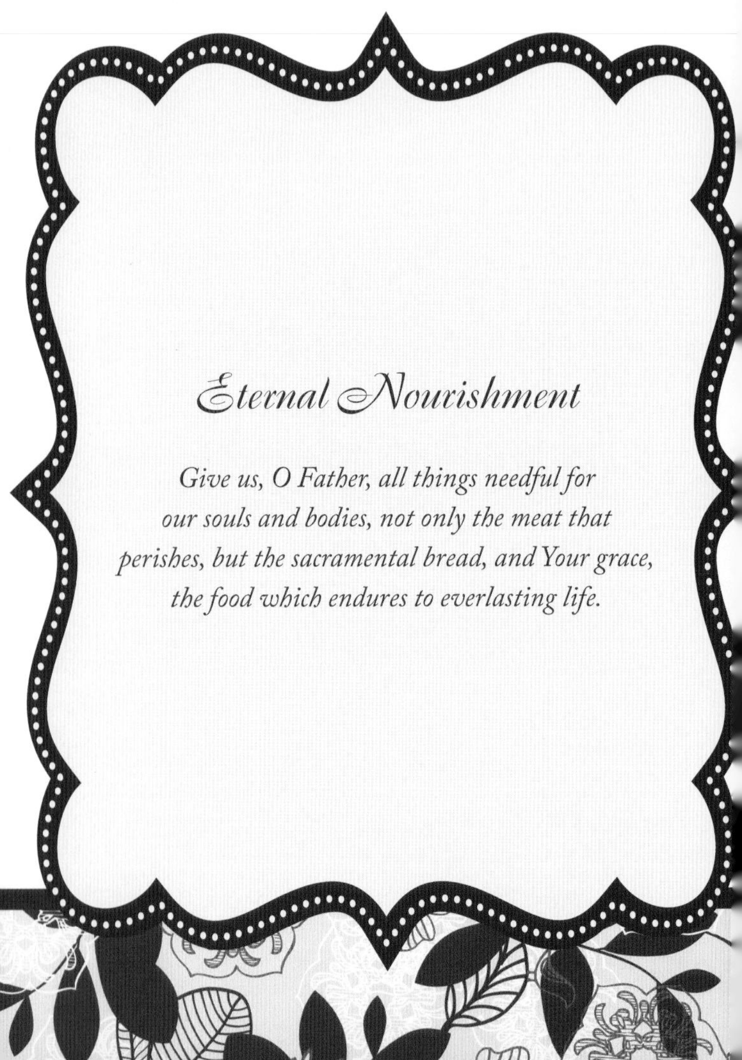

Eternal Nourishment

Give us, O Father, all things needful for our souls and bodies, not only the meat that perishes, but the sacramental bread, and Your grace, the food which endures to everlasting life.

The Never-Ending Resource

Prayer is. . .a mine which is never exhausted. . . .
It is the root, the fountain,
the mother of a thousand blessings.

—JOHN CHRYSOSTOM

Steady Blessings

"If you follow my decrees and are careful to obey
my commands, I will send you rain in its season,
and the ground will yield its crops and the trees of
the field their fruit. Your threshing will continue
until grape harvest and the grape harvest will
continue until planting, and you will eat all the
food you want and live in safety in your land."

—LEVITICUS 26:3–5 NIV

All That Is

All that is good, all that is true,
all that is beautiful, all that is beneficent,
be it great or small, be it perfect or fragmentary,
natural as well as supernatural, moral as
well as material, comes from God.

—JOHN NEWMAN

Memories

Memories are the treasures that we keep
locked deep within the storehouse of our souls,
to keep our hearts warm when we are lonely.

—BECKY ALIGADA

True Colors

God offers us His Spirit, not just as an encouragement, but as a heart-changer. He enters into us and begins to redesign our interior life. Suddenly our actions and our words are truthful, kind, and fair. No longer do they reflect the blackness that painted our hearts, but the rainbow colors of His blessings.

Hunger for Blessings

It seems to me we can never give up longing and wishing while we are alive. There are certain things we feel to be beautiful and good, and we must hunger for them.

—GEORGE ELIOT

True Bliss

The real joy of life is in its play.
Play is anything we do for the joy and love of
doing it, apart from any profit, compulsion,
or sense of duty. It is the real living of life.

—WALTER RAUSCHENBUSCH

No Worries

"Therefore I say to you, do not worry about your life, what you will eat; nor about the body, what you will put on. Life is more than food, and the body is more than clothing. Consider the ravens, for they neither sow nor reap, which have neither storehouse nor barn; and God feeds them. Of how much more value are you than the birds?"

—LUKE 12:22–24 NKJV

Go with God

May the road rise to meet you,
May the wind be always at your back,
May the sun shine warm upon your face,
May the rain fall soft upon your fields,
And, until we meet again,
May God hold you in the palm of His hand.

—IRISH BLESSING

Be Glad

Be glad of life, because it gives you the chance to love and to work and to play and to look up at the stars; to be satisfied with your possessions. . . to think seldom of your enemies, often of your friends, and every day of Christ.

—HENRY VAN DYKE

Never Apart

Would God give a sparrow all it needs for life and leave a human out of the loop? Obviously the Creator doesn't forget or ignore anything. Without Him, Earth wouldn't exist. The universe can't keep its course apart from His command. But sometimes we wonder if we've somehow disconnected from God. All along, God never forgets our needs.

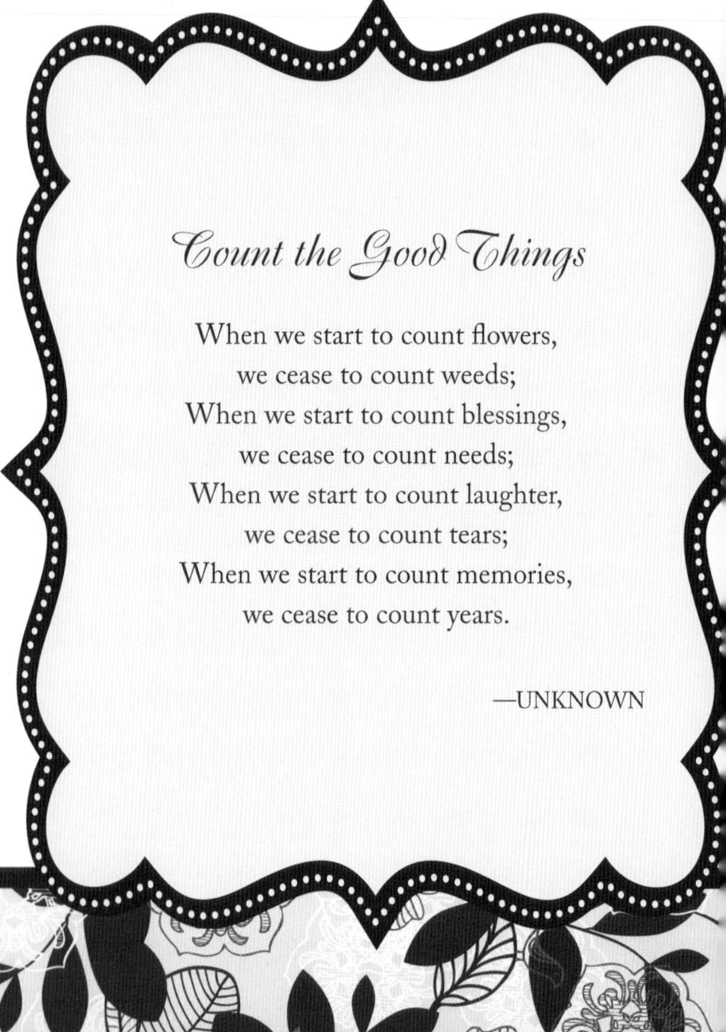

Count the Good Things

When we start to count flowers,
we cease to count weeds;
When we start to count blessings,
we cease to count needs;
When we start to count laughter,
we cease to count tears;
When we start to count memories,
we cease to count years.

—UNKNOWN

Bless Others

The Bible most often refers to human abilities as "gifts" because they are given in order to be given again. . . . God expects you to strengthen and polish [your gifts] and use [them] to enrich the lives of others. . . . As you use your gifts to bless others, you will be blessed most of all.

Bountiful Blessings

And God is able to make all grace abound to you, so that in all things at all times, having all that you need, you will abound in every good work. As it is written: "He has scattered abroad his gifts to the poor; his righteousness endures forever."

—2 CORINTHIANS 9:8–9 NIV

His Delightful Touch

The Lord gives you the experience of
enjoying His presence. He touches you,
and His touch is so delightful that,
more than ever, you are drawn inwardly to Him.

—JEANNE GUYON

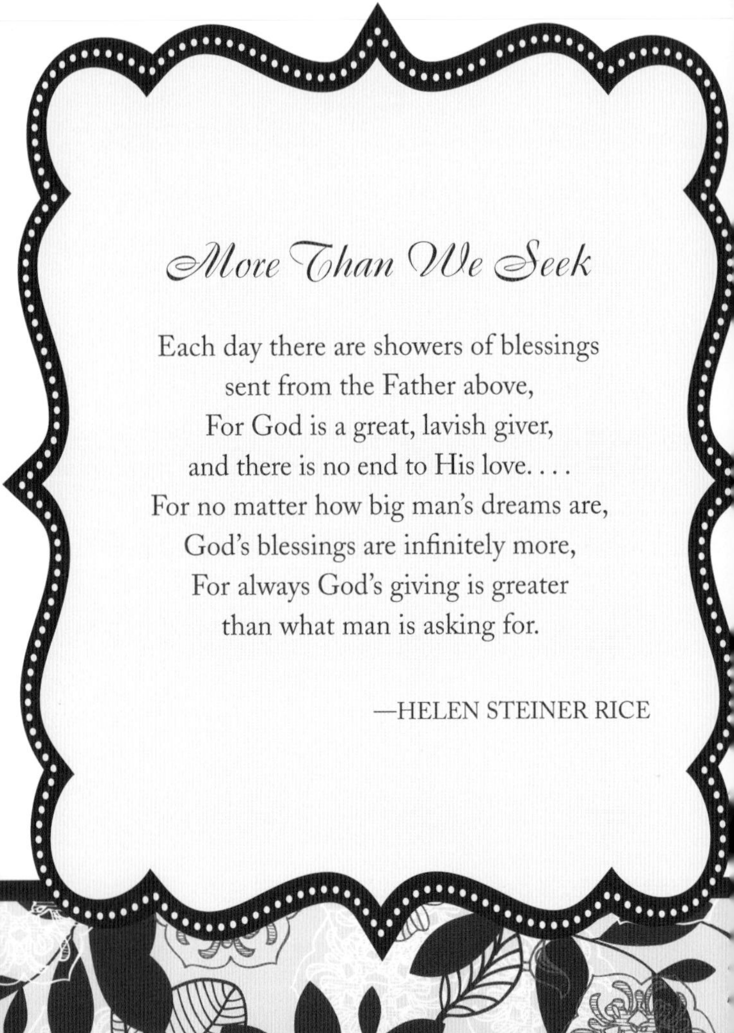

More Than We Seek

Each day there are showers of blessings
sent from the Father above,
For God is a great, lavish giver,
and there is no end to His love. . . .
For no matter how big man's dreams are,
God's blessings are infinitely more,
For always God's giving is greater
than what man is asking for.

—HELEN STEINER RICE

Slow Down!

Don't let yourself get so busy that you miss those little but important extras in life—the beauty of a day. . .the smile of a friend. . .the serenity of a quiet moment alone. For it is often life's smallest pleasures and gentlest joys that make the biggest and most lasting difference.

A Perfect Circle

A circle has no beginning and no ending. The circle of blessing can begin at any point within it. The circle is made up of quiet actions, love, simple gratitude, forgiveness, generous gifts, trust, precious memories, a heart that knows what to remember and what to forget.

—UNKNOWN

Now and Always

Father, thank You for all You have given me,
for all You have taught me, and for all
the good times still to come. Amen.

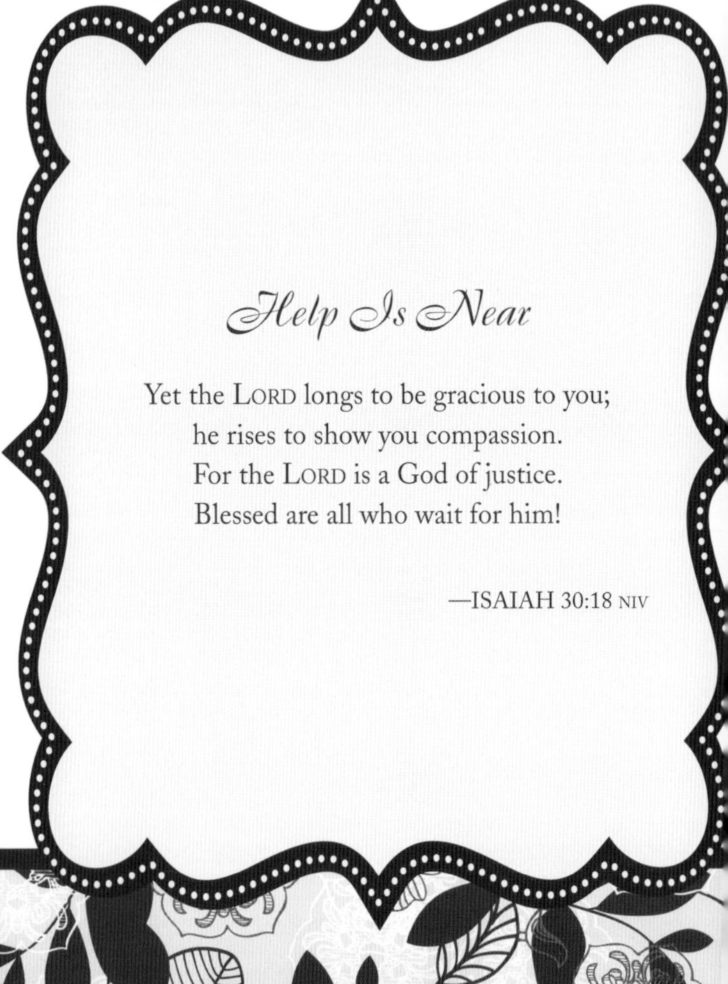

Help Is Near

Yet the Lord longs to be gracious to you;
he rises to show you compassion.
For the Lord is a God of justice.
Blessed are all who wait for him!

—ISAIAH 30:18 NIV

Bright Moments

Trust that any unclear moments will bring you to that moment of clarity and action when you are known by God and know Him. These are better and brighter moments of His blessing.

Relish the Good. . .and Bad

The marvelous richness of human experience would lose something of rewarding joy if there were no limitations to overcome. The hilltop hour would not be half so wonderful if there were no dark valleys to traverse.

—HELEN KELLER

The Greatest Promise

A rainbow stretches from one end of the sky to the other. Each shade of color, each facet of light, displays the radiant spectrum of God's love—a promise that He will always love each one of us at our worst and at our best.

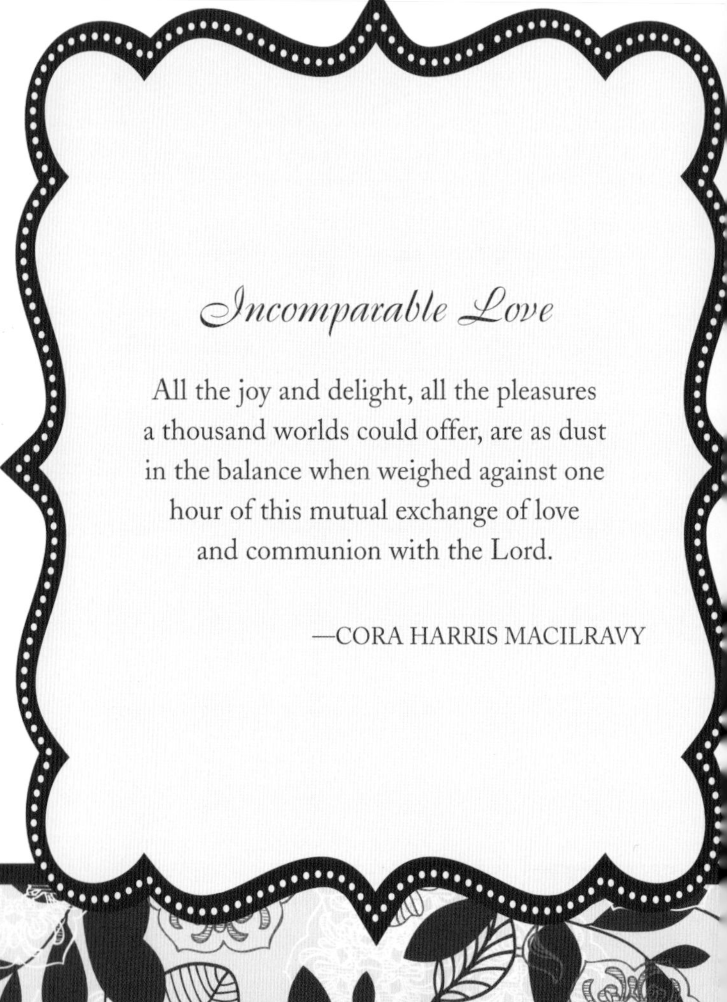

Incomparable Love

All the joy and delight, all the pleasures a thousand worlds could offer, are as dust in the balance when weighed against one hour of this mutual exchange of love and communion with the Lord.

—CORA HARRIS MACILRAVY

Beyond Our Asking

More than hearts can imagine or minds comprehend,
God's bountiful gifts are ours without end.
We ask for a cupful when the vast sea is ours.
We pick a small rosebud from a garden of flowers.
Whatever we ask for falls short of God's giving,
For His greatness exceeds every facet of living.

—HELEN STEINER RICE

Ask, Knock, Seek

"I say to you, ask, and what you ask for will be given to you. Look, and what you are looking for you will find. Knock, and the door you are knocking on will be opened to you. For everyone who asks, will receive what he asks for. Everyone who looks, will find what he is looking for. Everyone who knocks, will have the door opened to him."

—LUKE 11:9–10 NLV

Sweet Hour of Prayer

Sweet hour of prayer! Sweet hour of prayer!
The joys I feel, the bliss I share,
Of those whose anxious spirits burn
With strong desires for thy return!
With such I hasten to the place
Where God my Savior shows His face,
And gladly take my station there,
And wait for thee, sweet hour of prayer!

—WILLIAM WALFORD

Patient Faith

Dear Lord, thank You for my life and everything in it: the good, the bad, and all the future blessing that I know You'll send my way. Help me to recognize the trials in my life as Your gifts in disguise and to wait patiently as Your plan comes to fruition in my life. Amen.

A Steady Stream

Even in the midst of our worst troubles,
we can trust that, as Jesus said,
God still remembers how to give good gifts.
Though we may not like our situation,
God's ability to give good things hasn't dried up.

Our Father's World

Everywhere across the land
You see God's face and touch His hand.
Each time you look up in the sky
Or watch the fluffy clouds drift by,
Or hear a bluebird brightly sing,
Or see the winter turn to spring,
Or touch a leaf or see a tree,
It's all God whispering, "This is Me. . . ."

—HELEN STEINER RICE

Blessed Showers

The enormous wealth of love God has for you compels Him to shower you with His presence and draw you close to Him. The fresh scent that remains after a spring rain shower is an open invitation to rest in His mercy and grace. . .His gentle desire to satisfy your heart with everything good.

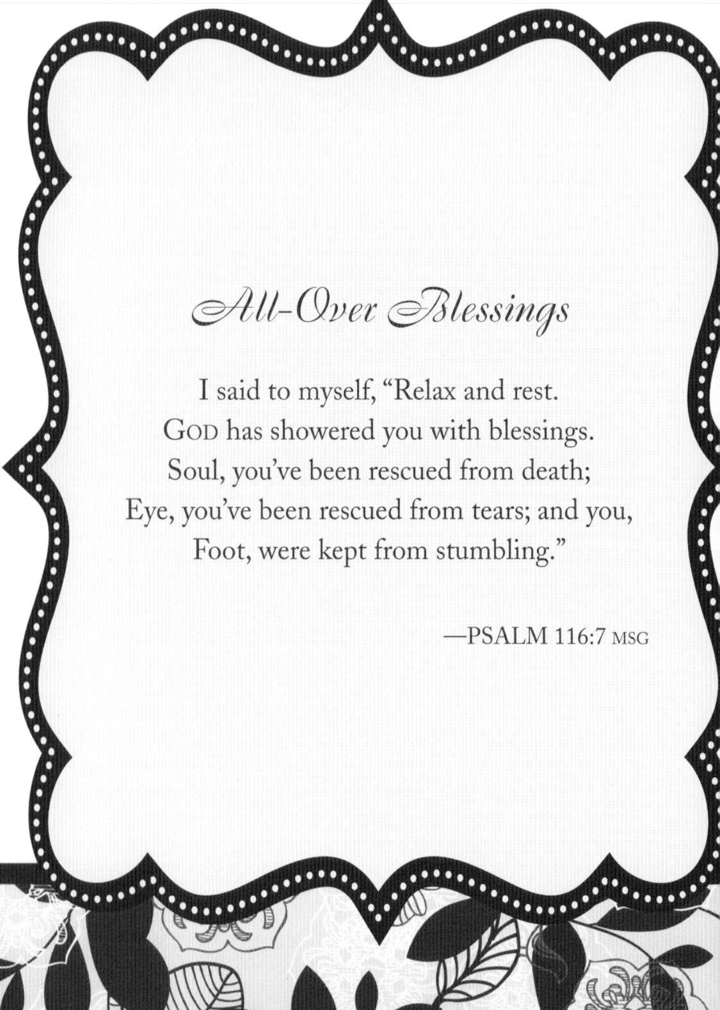

All-Over Blessings

I said to myself, "Relax and rest.
God has showered you with blessings.
Soul, you've been rescued from death;
Eye, you've been rescued from tears; and you,
Foot, were kept from stumbling."

—PSALM 116:7 MSG

Things to Come

If God hath made this world so fair,
Where sin and death abound,
How beautiful beyond compare
Will paradise be found!

—JAMES MONTGOMERY

Worldly Riches vs. God's Riches

Nothing more clearly shows how little God esteems His gift to men of wealth, money, position, and other worldly goods, than the way He distributes these, and the sort of men who are most amply provided with them.

—JEAN DE LA BRUYÈRE

Unconditional Love

A simple pleasure like the unconditional love of a dog reminds us that though we may stray, God always calls us back to the home of His heart.

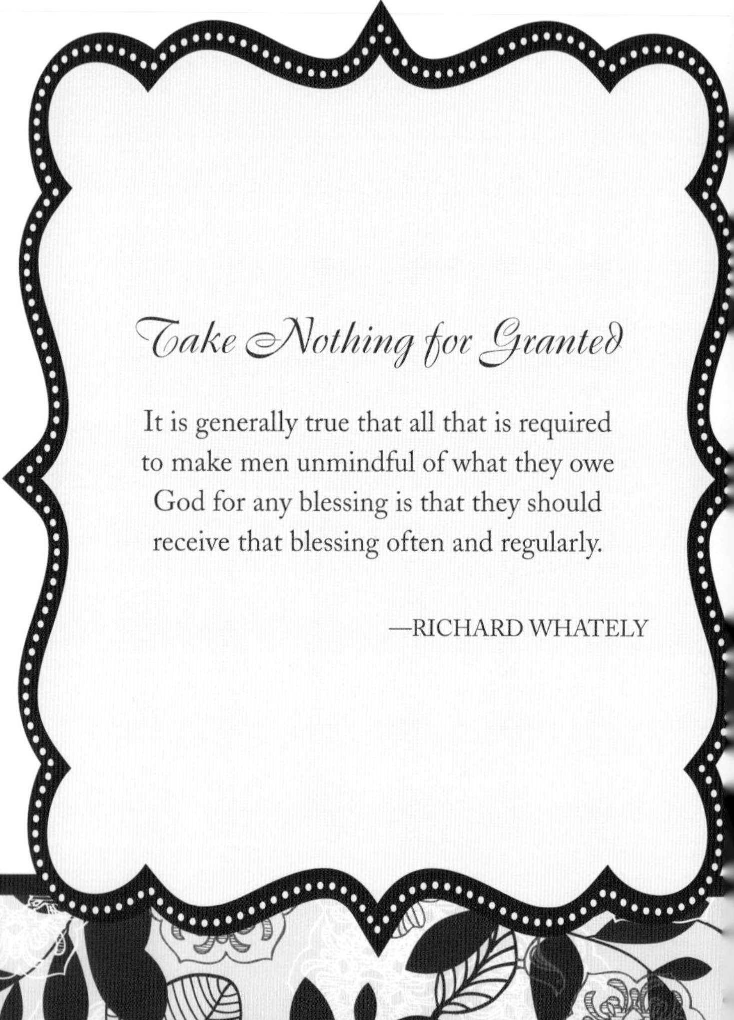

Take Nothing for Granted

It is generally true that all that is required to make men unmindful of what they owe God for any blessing is that they should receive that blessing often and regularly.

—RICHARD WHATELY

Joy and Righteousness

Our Lord has purchased joy, as well as righteousness, for us. It is the very design of the gospel that, being saved from guilt, we should be happy in the love of Christ.

The Source of Wealth

You may say to yourself, "My power and the strength of my hands have produced this wealth for me." But remember the Lord your God, for it is he who gives you the ability to produce wealth.

—DEUTERONOMY 8:17–18 NIV

God Cares

Father, Your correction lasts only a moment; but its blessings are eternal. When I realize You are so concerned for me and want to help me, I am filled with gratitude and willing to be led in the right direction. Amen.

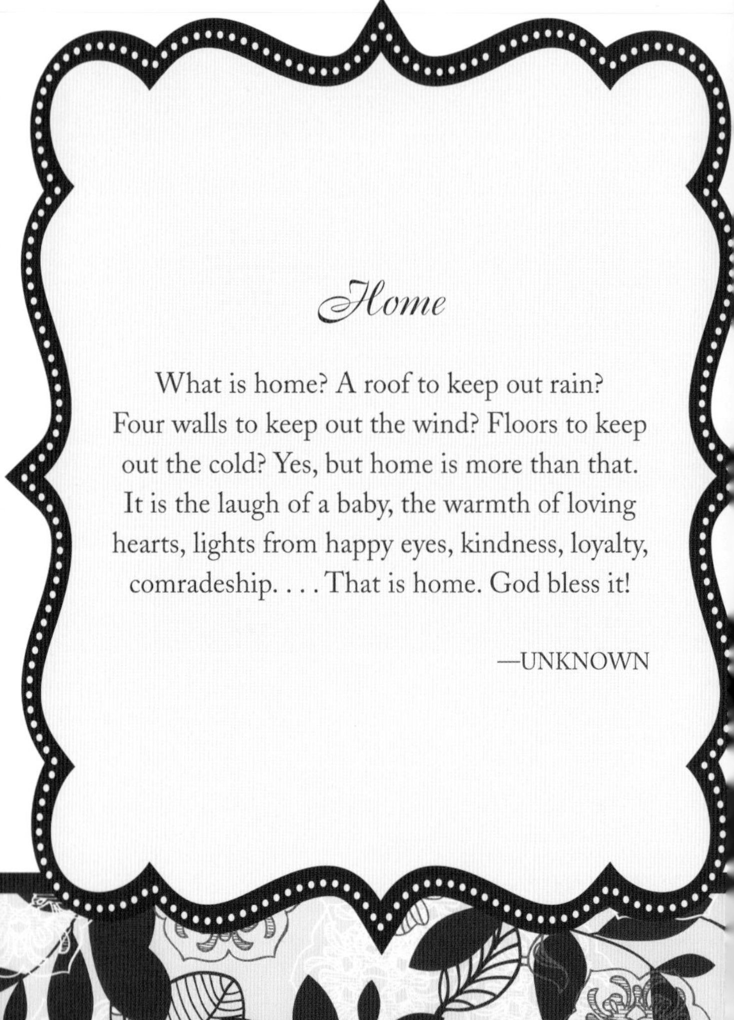

Home

What is home? A roof to keep out rain?
Four walls to keep out the wind? Floors to keep out the cold? Yes, but home is more than that. It is the laugh of a baby, the warmth of loving hearts, lights from happy eyes, kindness, loyalty, comradeship. . . . That is home. God bless it!

—UNKNOWN

God's Intention

When we thank God for His blessings and use them properly—to help others and support our families in a responsible Christian lifestyle—worldly goods become blessings He can use through us. That's just what God intended.

God's Bouquet

All the flowers God has made are beautiful.
The rose in its glory and the lily in its whiteness
do not rob the tiny violet of its sweet smell,
or the daisy of its charming simplicity.

—THÈRÉSE OF LISIEUX

Butterflies

Happiness is as a butterfly, which, when pursued,
is always beyond your grasp, but which,
if you will sit down quietly, may alight upon you.

—NATHANIEL HAWTHORNE

My whole being, praise the LORD and do not forget all his kindnesses. He forgives all my sins and heals all my diseases. He saves my life from the grave and loads me with love and mercy. He satisfies me with good things and makes me young again, like the eagle.

—PSALM 103:2–5 NCV

In the Valley of Love

'Tis a gift to be simple, 'tis a gift to be free,
'Tis a gift to come down where we ought to be—
And when we find ourselves in the place just right,
'Twill be in the valley of love and delight.

—SHAKER HYMN

Cherish

Cherish your visions; cherish your ideals; cherish the music that stirs in your heart, the beauty that forms in your mind, and the loveliness that drapes your purest thoughts, for out of them will grow all delightful conditions, all heavenly environment.

—JAMES ALLEN

A Wellspring of Hope

When we suffer, hope still springs up in us. As Christians we are especially able to continue anticipating the best, even when life tries to make us doubt it. Why? Because our hope is firmly set in the God of all grace, who has already showered us with blessings.

Joy

Joy is not in things;
it is in us.

—RICHARD WAGNER

Health vs. Money

There is this difference between the two temporal blessings—health and money; money is the most envied, but the least enjoyed; health is the most enjoyed, but the least envied; and this superiority of the latter is still more obvious when we reflect.

—CHARLES CALEB COLTON

Acclaim Him!

Blessed are those who have learned to acclaim you,
who walk in the light of your presence, O Lord.
They rejoice in your name all day long;
they exult in your righteousness.

—PSALM 89:15–16 NIV

Wildflower Virtues

We complicate our lives when we borrow trouble from the future. . . . We miss the precious gift of peace that God has given us right here, right now, in this tiny present moment that touches eternity. Be like the wildflowers. . . simply soaking up today's sunshine.

—ELLYN SANNA

A Song at Daybreak

O God, great and wonderful, who has created the heavens, dwelling in the light and beauty of it; who has made the earth, revealing Yourself in every flower that opens; let not my eyes be blind to You, neither my heart be dead, but teach me to praise You, even as the lark, which offers her song at daybreak.

—ISIDORE OF SEVILLE

Perfect Gifts

Don't judge God's gifts until you've unwrapped the whole package. Often His presents are larger than they seem and take longer to unpack than you thought. But in the end, you're likely to learn that whatever pain you put into the situation is much less than His blessing. . . . God's gifts are perfect after all.

Unprompted Blessings

God, who is love. . .simply cannot help but shed blessing on blessing upon us. We do not need to beg, for He simply cannot help it!

—HANNAH WHITALL SMITH

The Best Mold

One of God's richest blessings. . .is that our children come into the world as people we're supposed to guide and direct, and then God uses them to form us—if we will only listen.

—DENA DYER

A Joyful Reward

Sons are a heritage from the Lord, children a reward from him. Like arrows in the hands of a warrior are sons born in one's youth.

—PSALM 127:3–4 NIV

Special Deliveries

God sends us children. . .to enlarge our hearts,
to make us unselfish and full of kindly sympathies
and affections, to give our souls higher aims. . .
to bring round our fireside bright faces and
happy smiles, and loving, tender hearts.

—MARY HOWITT

Choose to Rejoice

It is no use to grumble and complain;
It's just as cheap and easy to rejoice;
When God sorts out the weather
and sends rain—
Why, rain's my choice.

—JAMES WHITCOMB RILEY

Normal Day

Normal day, let me be aware of the treasure you are. Let me learn from you, love you, bless you before you depart. Let me not pass you by in quest of some rare and perfect tomorrow.

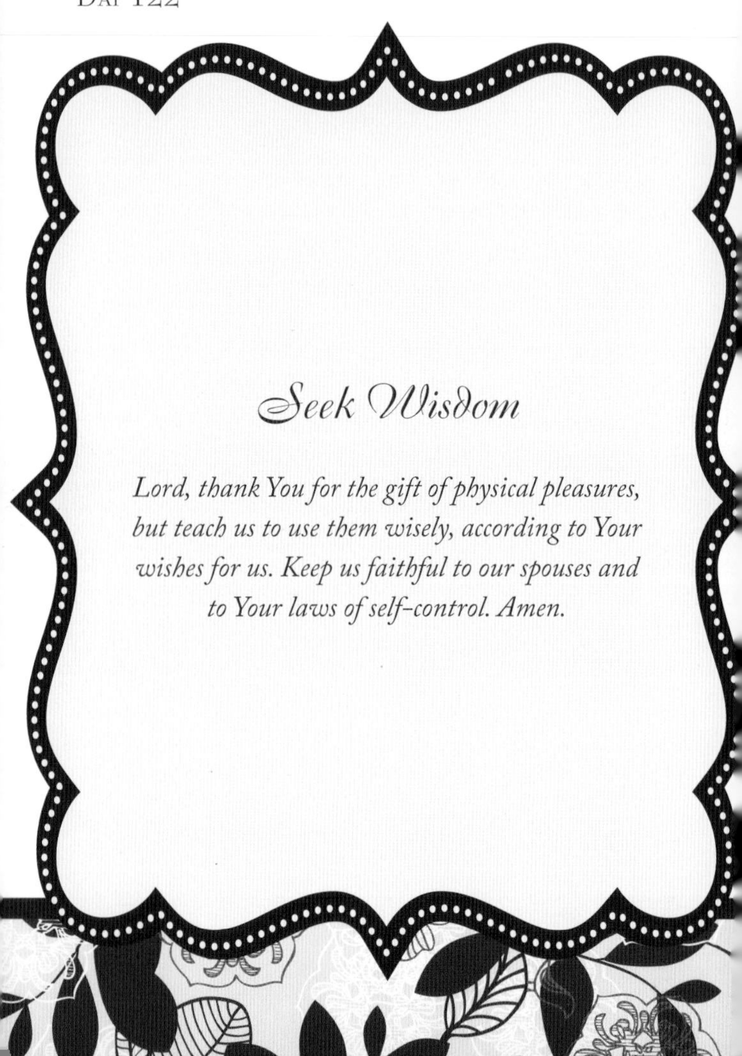

Seek Wisdom

Lord, thank You for the gift of physical pleasures, but teach us to use them wisely, according to Your wishes for us. Keep us faithful to our spouses and to Your laws of self-control. Amen.

A United Household

May [God] grant you all the things which your heart desires, and may [He] give you a [spouse] and a home and gracious concord, for there is nothing greater and better than this—when a husband and wife keep a household in oneness of mind—a great woe to their enemies and joy to their friends—and win high renown.

—HOMER

Never Separated

For I am convinced that neither death nor life, neither angels nor demons, neither the present nor the future, nor any powers, neither height nor depth, nor anything else in all creation, will be able to separate us from the love of God that is in Christ Jesus our Lord.

—ROMANS 8:38–39 NIV

Natural Wonders

The wonder of living is held within the beauty
of silence, the glory of sunlight, the sweetness
of fresh spring air, the quiet strength of earth,
and the love that lies at the very root of all things.

—UNKNOWN

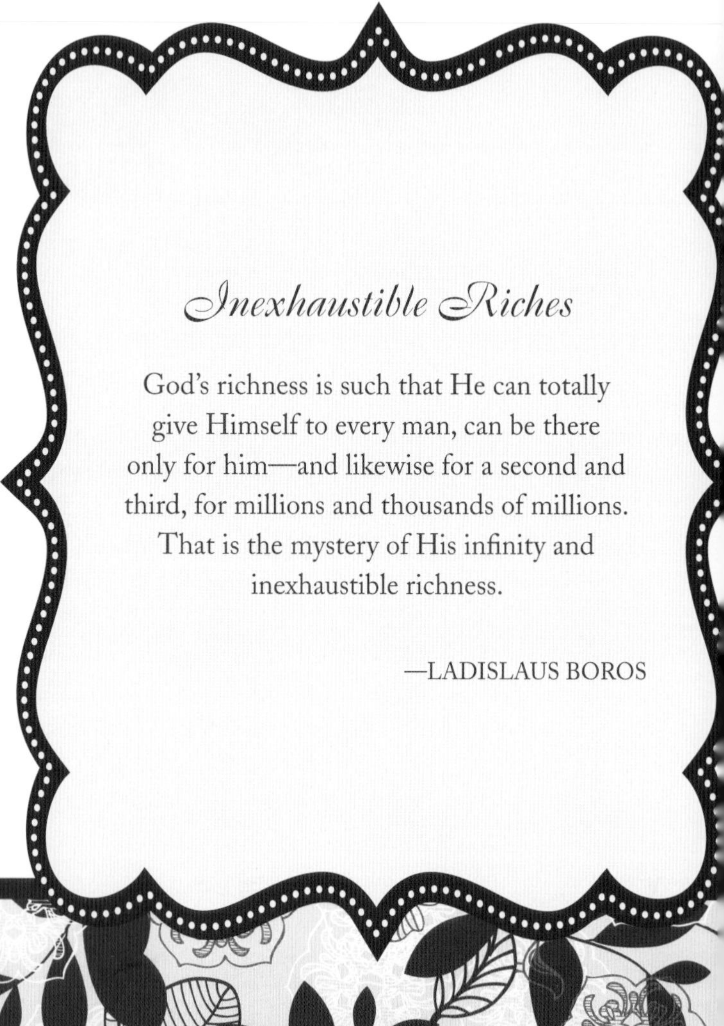

Inexhaustible Riches

God's richness is such that He can totally give Himself to every man, can be there only for him—and likewise for a second and third, for millions and thousands of millions. That is the mystery of His infinity and inexhaustible richness.

—LADISLAUS BOROS

His Marvelous Creation

Have you ever looked at God's stars and marveled as they lit the velvet-dark sky? Watched a sunset in which the sky was tinted from the lightest blue on the horizon to a deep tone above and delighted in God's paintbrush? Then you've seen Him make things beautiful in their time.

His Unfailing Love

"Though mountains be shaken and the hills be removed, yet my unfailing love for you will not be shaken nor my covenant of peace be removed," says the Lord, who has compassion on you.

—ISAIAH 54:10 NIV

May

The word *May* is a perfumed word. . . . It means youth, love, song, and all that is beautiful in life.

—HENRY WADSWORTH LONGFELLOW

Take Heart

"Blessed are you when men hate you,
when they exclude you and insult you and reject
your name as evil, because of the Son of Man."

—LUKE 6:22 NIV

A Song of Thanksgiving

You bless my life in many ways every day, Father. May I receive Your blessings with a song of thanksgiving on my lips. Amen.

Simple Blessings

To find the universal elements enough; to find the air and water exhilarating; to be refreshed by a morning walk or an evening saunter. . .to be thrilled by the stars at night; to be elated over a bird's nest or a wildflower in spring—these are some of the rewards of the simple life.

—JOHN BURROUGHS

Never Lacking

God's goodness and mercy come in many packages and many sizes, but they follow us each day of our existence. Whether we've passed through many hard times or just a few, no day given to any believer following Jesus lacks these two blessings.

Nothing hurts so much as dissatisfaction with our circumstances. . . . God knows what He is doing, and there is nothing accidental in the life of the believer. Nothing but good can come to those who are wholly His.

—WATCHMAN NEE

Small Pleasures

Happiness consists more in small conveniences or pleasures that occur every day than in the great pieces of good fortune that happen but seldom to a man in the course of his life.

—BENJAMIN FRANKLIN

Day 136

Filled with Laughter

Our mouths were filled with laughter, our tongues with songs of joy. Then it was said among the nations, "The Lord has done great things for them." The Lord has done great things for us, and we are filled with joy.

—PSALM 126:2–3 NIV

We Thank Thee

For health and food, for love and friends,
for everything Thy goodness sends,
Father in heaven, we thank Thee.

—RALPH WALDO EMERSON

Family Gifts

Families give us many things—
love and meaning, purpose and an
opportunity to give, and a sense of humor.

—UNKNOWN

His Child

You are God's child. That might seem a rather ordinary thing, but consider it more carefully, and feel the amazement of that truth. The Creator of the universe, the all-powerful God, wants to be your daddy (after all, that's what *Abba* means). This awesome being wants you to trust Him and seek His love and protection.

No Fear

We walk without fear, full of hope
and courage and strength to do His will,
waiting for the endless good which He is always
giving as fast as He can get us able to take it in.

—GEORGE MACDONALD

Less Is More

Fear less, hope more; eat less, chew more; whine less, breathe more; talk less, say more; love more, and all good things will be yours.

—SWEDISH PROVERB

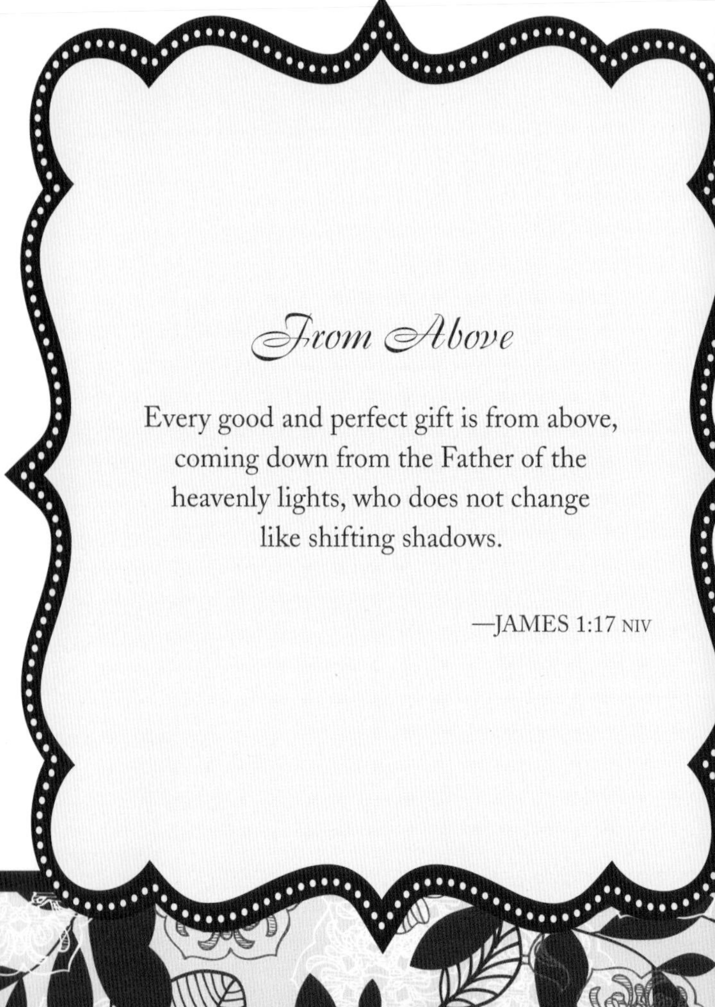

From Above

Every good and perfect gift is from above, coming down from the Father of the heavenly lights, who does not change like shifting shadows.

—JAMES 1:17 NIV

Focus on the Present

Lord, help me to rejoice in the time I have with my family today. I don't want to dwell on what might happen in the future; I want to relish this chance to nurture and cherish the blessings You've given me. Amen.

Give Love

Love is the greatest thing that God can give us; for He Himself is love; and it is the greatest thing we can give to God.

—JEREMY TAYLOR

Our Heavenly Weatherman

The weather is not ours to control, but God's. We need to give thanks for the daily blessings God offers us—rain that keeps wells and reservoirs filled or sunshine for a special outing. When the weather doesn't go "our way," we can still thank God that He's in control.

God Is Good

The joyful birds prolong the strain, their songs with every spring renewed; the air we breathe, and the falling rain, each softly whispers: God is good.

—JOHN HAMPDEN GURNEY

Common Miracles

The miracles of nature do not seem miraculous because they are so common. If no one had ever seen a flower, even a dandelion would be the most startling event in the world.

—UNKNOWN

Blessed Are You

"Blessed are the poor in spirit, for theirs is the kingdom of heaven. Blessed are those who mourn, for they shall be comforted. Blessed are the meek, for they shall inherit the earth. Blessed are those who hunger and thirst for righteousness, for they shall be satisfied."

—MATTHEW 5:3–6 ESV

Find a Path

The means in which different people are led, and in which they find the blessing of God, are varied, transposed, and combined together a thousand different ways.

A Sense of Beautiful

A person should hear a little music, read a little poetry, and see a fine picture every day of their life, in order that worldly cares may not obliterate the sense of beautiful which God has implanted in the human soul.

—JOHANN WOLFGANG VON GOETHE

Excellent Things!

Excellent things! God doesn't just do good things or the best things. He does excellent things. What could improve on God's superb plan or will? Are our eyes open to the excellent things He's done for His people—and is still doing for them today?

Awesome Landscapes

Dear Lord, we give You thanks for the bright silent moon, and thanks for the sun that will warm us at noon. And thanks for the stars and the quick running breeze, and thanks for the shade and straightness of trees. Amen.

Incomprehensible Love

We are so preciously loved by God that we cannot even comprehend it. No created being can ever know how much and how sweetly and tenderly God loves them.

—JULIAN OF NORWICH

His Beloved Earth

You care for the land and water it; you enrich it abundantly. The streams of God are filled with water to provide the people with grain, for so you have ordained it. You drench its furrows and level its ridges; you soften it with showers and bless its crops.

—PSALM 65:9–10 NIV

In His Footsteps

When someone does a kindness,
It always seems to me
That's the way God up in heaven
Would like us all to be.
For when we follow in His footsteps
I'm very sure it's true
That in serving those around us,
We serve and please God, too.

—HELEN STEINER RICE

Time

Let me tell thee, time is a very precious gift from God; so precious that it's only given to us moment by moment.

—AMELIA BARR

Our Needs Fulfilled

God's blessings begin with the spiritual, but they don't end there. As God recognizes the needs of this world, we should, too. Often it's the body's needs that make people aware of spiritual emptiness. God deals with every phase of our lives, and as we offer Jesus to others, we can do that, too.

Open Your Heart

The best and most beautiful things in the world cannot be seen or even touched. They must be felt with the heart.

—HELEN KELLER

Overflowing Beauty

The full woods overflow
among the meadow's gold!
A bluebell wave has rolled,
where crowded cowslips grow.
The drifting hawthorn snow
brims over hill and world.
The full woods overflow
among the meadow's gold. . . .
Heaven's beauty crowds below,
the full woods overflow!

—MARY WEBB

God's Plan

And this is God's plan: Both Gentiles and Jews who believe the Good News share equally in the riches inherited by God's children. Both are part of the same body, and both enjoy the promise of blessings because they belong to Christ Jesus.

—EPHESIANS 3:6 NLT

Finding the Good

You may tend to think of God gratefully in the good times and ask for His help in the bad. But sometimes you have to consider that God brings good out of both. No matter what your feelings tell you, you can trust Him to work out His purpose in you at all times.

Blessed Security

Lord, I thank You for Your guidance and protection day after day. Although I never know what the day will bring, You have a plan, and I trust in You. Amen.

Yours for the Taking

"It's for you I created the universe" [says God]. "I love you. There's only one catch. Like any other gift, the gift of grace can be yours only if you'll reach out and take it." Maybe being able to reach out and take it is a gift, too.

—FREDRICK BUECHNER

No More Yearning

In all ranks of life the human heart yearns for the beautiful; and the beautiful things that God makes are His gift to all alike.

—HARRIET BEECHER STOWE

Humor

Humor is the great thing, the saving thing. The minute it crops up, all our irritations and resentments slip away and a sunny spirit takes their place.

—MARK TWAIN

God Bless You

"The Lord bless you and keep you;
the Lord make his face shine upon you
and be gracious to you; the Lord turn his
face toward you and give you peace."

—NUMBERS 6:24–26 NIV

Rest Assured

Rest is not idleness, and to lie sometimes on the grass under trees on a summer's day, listening to the murmur of the water, or watching the clouds float across the sky, is by no means a waste of time.

—SIR JOHN LUBBOCK

Relax!

God provides resting places as well as working places. Rest, then, and be thankful when He brings you, wearied, to a wayside well.

—L. B. COWMAN

Family Time

Thank You for my home, dear Jesus. I just love to be here. I can't explain the joy that comes from being surrounded by those I love. Whether our home is filled with laughter during game night or shrouded in silent contemplation during family devotions, I can feel Your presence, and I am uplifted.

Uncut Diamonds

Guard well your spare moments. They are like uncut diamonds. Discard them and their value will never be known. Improve them and they will become the brightest gems in a useful life.

—RALPH WALDO EMERSON

A Light in the Dark

For many people, the heavy responsibilities of home and family and earning a living absorb all their time and strength. Yet such a home—where love is—may be a light shining in a dark place, a silent witness to the reality and love of God.

—OLIVE WYON

Little in Return

He has showed you, O man, what is good.
And what does the Lord require of you?
To act justly and to love mercy and to
walk humbly with your God.

—MICAH 6:8 NIV

Friends Are a Gift

Dear God, thank You for my friends. Help me not to take them for granted. . . . Remind me often how poor my life would be without the friends You've given me. Help me to enrich their live as they have mine. Amen.

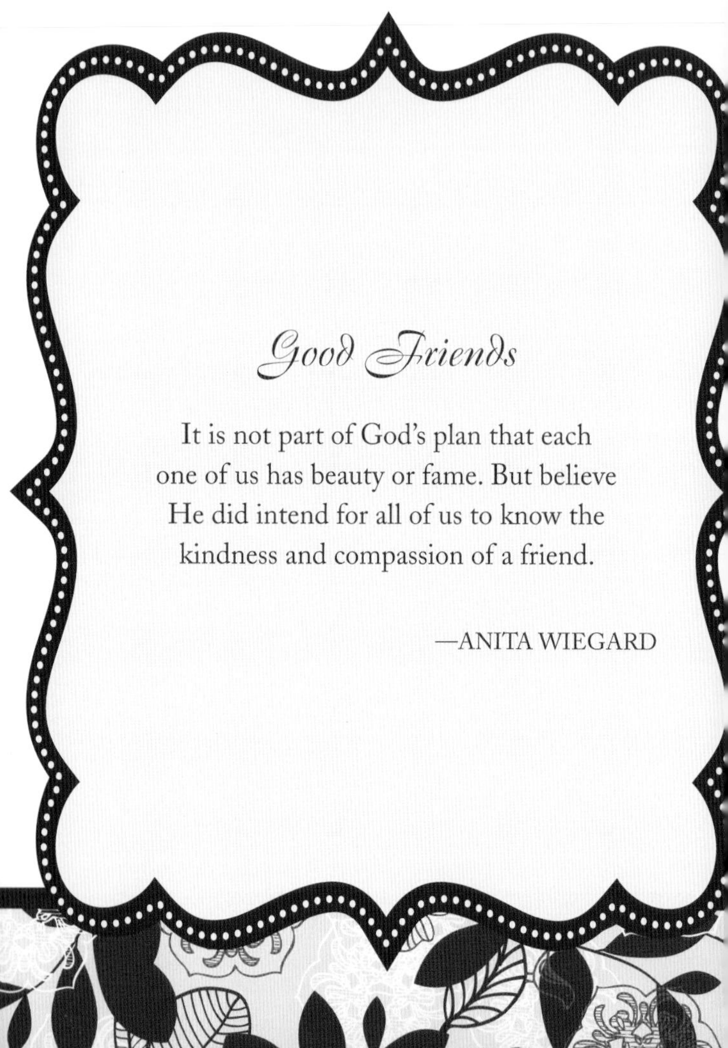

Good Friends

It is not part of God's plan that each one of us has beauty or fame. But believe He did intend for all of us to know the kindness and compassion of a friend.

—ANITA WIEGARD

Our Mission

By placing us in this world, God has given us a mission, and prayer is a part of it. By lifting others up to Him, we take part in the blessing He bestows upon the world. Just as Jesus won't forget us, we need to remember those whose lives we touch. Because we know Jesus, we can pray effectively—and perhaps that's the most potent impact we'll have on another's life.

The Spiritual Lesson of Pain

How little we know what God has in store
As daily He blesses our lives more and more.
For pain has a way of broadening our view
And bringing us closer in sympathy, too.
For none of us knows what pain is all about
Until our spiritual wings start to sprout.

—HELEN STEINER RICE

An Inhabited Garden

The world is so empty if one thinks only of the mountains, rivers, and cities; but to know someone here and there who thinks and feels with us, and who, though distant, is close to us in spirit, this makes the earth for us an inhabited garden.

—JOHANN WOLFGANG VON GOETHE

Bless Others

God has given each of you a gift.
Use it to help each other. This will
show God's loving-favor.

—1 PETER 4:10 NLV

Gift of Friendship

Blessed are they who have the gift of making friends, for it is one of God's best gifts. It involves many things, but above all, the power of going out of one's self and appreciating what is noble and loving in another.

—THOMAS HUGHES

Faithful Companionship

Dear God, thank You for understanding friends. Thank You that so often we're on the same wavelength, laughing together, crying together, encouraging each other with our understanding. I'm grateful that I'm not alone, that I can share my life with my friends. Amen.

We're Never Lost

God's blessings are available to even the most disobedient child who turns from sin. Pray for that loved one to turn and accept the Savior's love. Over and over God gave that blessing to Israel. He'll give it to those you love, too.

A Pretty Good World

Take one thing with another, and the world is a pretty good sort of world, and it is our duty to make the best of it and be thankful.

—BENJAMIN FRANKLIN

Youthful Joy

When the voices of children
Are heard on the green
And laughing is heard on the hill,
My heart is at rest within my breast
And everything else is still.

—WILLIAM BLAKE

An Outpouring of Blessing

"For I will pour water on the thirsty land, and streams on the dry ground; I will pour my Spirit upon your offspring, and my blessing on your descendants."

—ISAIAH 44:3 ESV

He Is Always Near

What other nation is so great as to have their
gods near them the way the Lord our God
is near us whenever we pray to him?

—DEUTERONOMY 4:7 NIV

Small Wonders

Everything has its wonders, even darkness and silence, and I learn, whatever state I am in, therein to be content.

—HELEN KELLER

Nothing Unappreciated

God doesn't promise to give all we want in a moment. The Christian walk is one of asking, seeking, knocking. God wants us to value the gifts He gives, and anything received too easily is also easily despised. Though He gives wholeheartedly and offers only the best, Jesus will have nothing unappreciated.

Blessed Prayer

Love to pray—feel often during the day
the need for prayer, and take trouble to pray.
Prayer enlarges the heart until it is capable
of containing God's gift of Himself.

—MOTHER TERESA

Unending Grace

The grace you had yesterday will not be sufficient for today. Grace is the overflowing favor of God, and you can always count on it being available to draw upon as needed.

—OSWALD CHAMBERS

God Grants Strength

But those who hope in the LORD will renew their strength. They will soar on wings like eagles; they will run and not grow weary, they will walk and not be faint.

—ISAIAH 40:31 NIV

Ask for Wisdom

Perseverance must finish its work so that you may be mature and complete, not lacking anything. If any of you lacks wisdom, he should ask God, who gives generously to all without finding fault, and it will be given to him. But when he asks, he must believe and not doubt, because he who doubts is like a wave of the sea, blown and tossed by the wind.

—JAMES 1:4–6 NIV

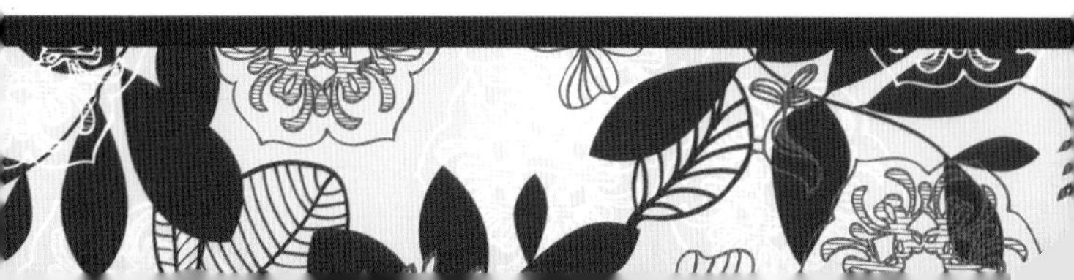

The Holy Spirit

Lord, one of the greatest gifts You've given me is the Holy Spirit to intercede for me during prayer. Thank You, Holy Spirit, for intervening and making my requests better than I ever could. Amen.

Wonderful Answers

When we hope for an awesome response to our communication with God, it's not because we're so wonderful. Finding the perfect way to ask won't work—that's expecting magic, not faith. But somehow, as we do our ordinary petitioning, God provides the wonderful answers.

Do not spoil what you have by desiring what you have not; but remember that what you now have was once among the things only hoped for.

—EPICURUS

Ever-Present Blessings

When I called upon God to show Himself
to me, He blessed me with. . .a letter bearing
good news, a caring voice on the phone,
a forgiving heart, an invitation to share a cup
of tea. . .a knock at the door, a new beginning.
God showed Himself through friends,
both old and new. I am blessed once more!

—UNKNOWN

Live God's Way

But what happens when we live God's way?
He brings gifts into our lives, much the same
way that fruit appears in an orchard—things like
affection for others, exuberance about life, serenity.

—GALATIANS 5:22 MSG

Thanks and Praise

If anyone would tell you the shortest,
surest way to happiness and all perfection,
he must tell you to make it a rule to yourself to
thank and praise God for everything that happens
to you. For it is certain that whatever seeming
calamity happens to you, if you thank and praise
God for it, you turn it into a blessing.

—William Law

True Happiness

True happiness comes when we stop complaining about all the troubles we have and offer thanks for all the troubles we don't have.

—UNKNOWN

God's Delight

I imagine God delights in watching us take on new things, enjoy the world He's created for us, and learn more of Him. He created us because He wanted to share things with us, not only in eternity, but here on earth, too. Scripture contains frequent indications of the joy He has in His creation, and part of that creation is us.

Open Doors

When one door closes, another one opens, but we often look so long and regretfully at the closed door that we fail to see the one that has opened for us.

—ALEXANDER GRAHAM BELL

Small Joys

It isn't the great big pleasures that count the most;
it's making a great deal out of the little ones.

—JEAN WEBSTER

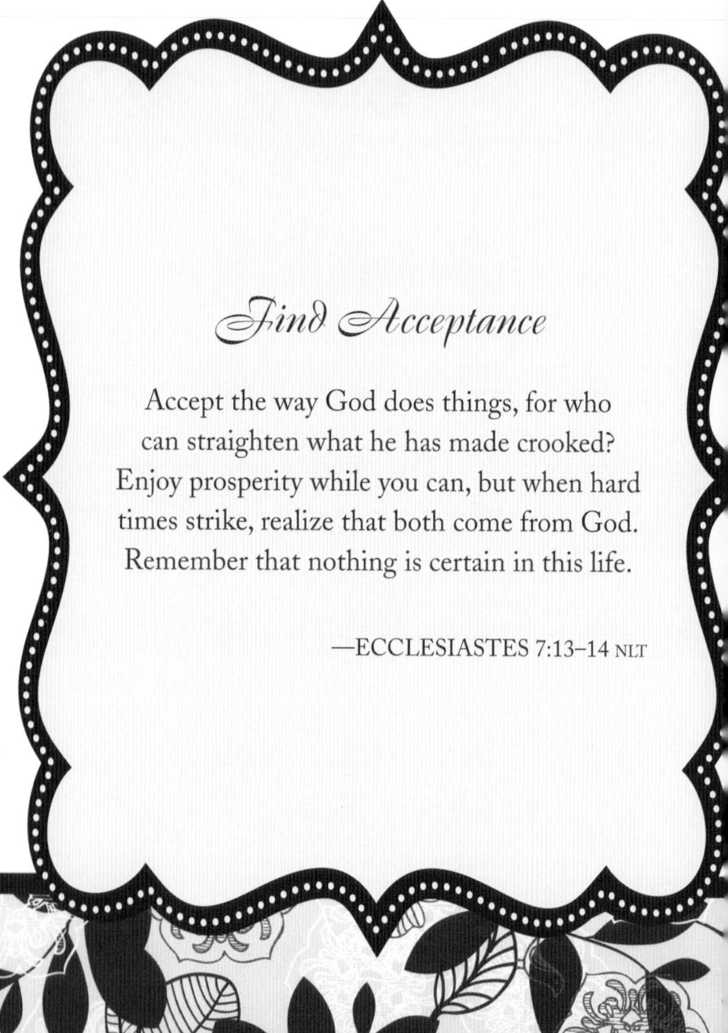

Find Acceptance

Accept the way God does things, for who can straighten what he has made crooked? Enjoy prosperity while you can, but when hard times strike, realize that both come from God. Remember that nothing is certain in this life.

—ECCLESIASTES 7:13–14 NLT

Walk with Him

May your footsteps set you upon a lifetime journey of love. May you wake each day with His blessings and sleep each night in His keeping. And may you always walk in His tender care.

The Rewards of Diligence

God's best gifts, like valuable jewels, are kept under
lock and key, and those who want them must,
with fervent faith, importunately ask for them;
for God is a rewarder of them
that diligently seek Him.

—D. L. MOODY

No Need to Wait

If you've been waiting for heaven to enjoy all the joys and delights of faith, turn around. Look at the blessings you've received today, all the things God has done and is doing in your life, and appreciate them. But don't stop there; you can also start taking advantage of the spiritual mission God has given you. Because God never gives us blessings simply to enjoy—every good thing is meant to be shared.

Limitless Hope

When we take time to notice the simple things in life, we never lack for encouragement. We discover we are surrounded by limitless hope that's just wearing everyday clothes.

—UNKNOWN

A Splendid Gift

Live your life while you have it.
Life is a splendid gift—
there is nothing small about it.

—FLORENCE NIGHTINGALE

Our Safe-Covering

For the Lord God is a sun and shield; the Lord bestows favor and honor; no good thing does he withhold from those whose walk is blameless.

—PSALM 84:11 NIV

Beyond All Profusion

I know nothing so pleasant as to sit there on a summer afternoon, with the western sun flickering through the great eldertree. . .where flowers and flowering shrubs are set as thick as grass in a field, a wilderness blossom, interwoven, intertwined, wreathy, garland, profuse beyond all profusion.

—MARY RUSSELL MITFORD

Day 210

Great beauty, great strength, and great riches are really and truly of no great use; a right heart exceeds all.

—BENJAMIN FRANKLIN

Kind Words

One of the greatest blessings of the Christian life is a kind word, spoken just when you need to hear it. Caring kindness should set Christians apart from unbelievers.

Relish Your Happiness

Thank You, Lord, for what I do have, which is happiness. Help me be wise with what money I have and use it in a way that pleases You. Amen.

Fresh Blessings

If God grants still to pour fresh blessings upon us, yes, even the greatest of all blessings, salvation, what can we say to these things but, "Thanks be to God for His unspeakable gift!"

A Gentle Shepherd

The Lord is my shepherd, I shall not be in want. He makes me lie down in green pastures, he leads me beside quiet waters, he restores my soul. He guides me in paths of righteousness for his name's sake. . . . You prepare a table before me in the presence of my enemies. You anoint my head with oil; my cup overflows.

—PSALM 23:1–3, 5 NIV

We Need Him

God does not give us everything we want, but He does fulfill all His promises. . .leading us along the best and straightest paths to Himself.

—DIETRICH BONHOEFFER

Your Success

If the day and the night are such that you greet them with joy, and life emits a fragrance like flowers and sweet-scented herbs, is more elastic, more starry, more immortal—that is your success.

—HENRY DAVID THOREAU

No Flyaways

God doesn't expect His people to trust in flyaway blessings, when they can have the very best. He offers Himself as security for this life and eternity. Why would anyone choose anything less?

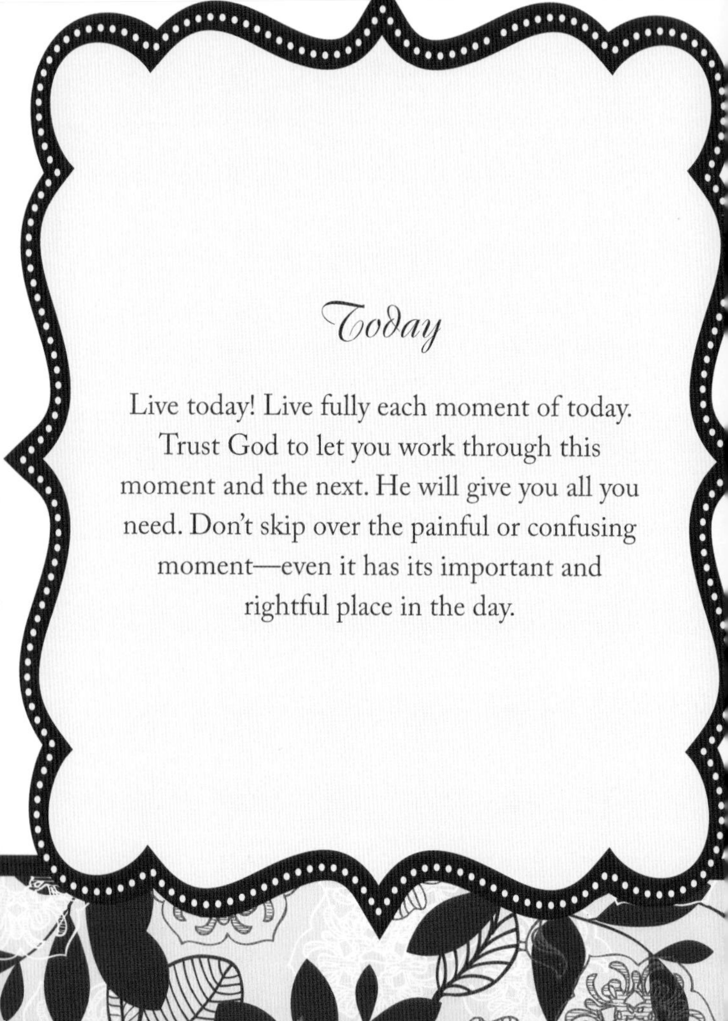

Today

Live today! Live fully each moment of today. Trust God to let you work through this moment and the next. He will give you all you need. Don't skip over the painful or confusing moment—even it has its important and rightful place in the day.

Happy Charities

The happiness of life is made up of minute fractions—the little, soon-forgotten charities of a kiss or a smile, a kind look, or heartfelt compliment.

—SAMUEL TAYLOR COLERIDGE

Ready to Give

"So if you sinful people know how to give good gifts to your children, how much more will your heavenly Father give the Holy Spirit to those who ask him."

—LUKE 11:13 NLT

The Very Best

Our Creator never would have made such lovely days, and have given us the deep hearts to enjoy them, above and beyond all thought, unless we were meant to be immortal.

—NATHANIEL HAWTHORNE

Abundant Blessings

However many blessings we expect from God,
His infinite liberality will always exceed
all our wishes and our thoughts.

—JOHN CALVIN

Good Intentions

Abundant life, full of good things on this earth—spiritual peace and joy, and full, satisfying relationships—that's what God intends His people to have. Because Jesus entered your life, you've entered a new realm. Life has taken on a new meaning, because you know the Creator.

Three Welcomes

May you always find three welcomes in life:
in a garden during summer, at a fireside
during winter, and whatever the day or
season in the kind eyes of a friend.

Spread the Love

Your heart is beating with God's love; open it to others. He has entrusted you with gifts and talents; use them for His service. He goes before you each step of the way; walk in faith. Take courage. Step out into the unknown with the One who knows all.

—ELLYN SANNA

The Rainbow

"I have set my rainbow in the clouds, and it will be the sign of the covenant between me and the earth. Whenever I bring clouds over the earth and the rainbow appears in the clouds, I will remember my covenant between me and you and all living creatures of every kind. Never again will the waters become a flood to destroy all life."

—GENESIS 9:13–15 NIV

Keep Watch

Be on the lookout for mercies. The more we look for them, the more of them we will see. Blessings brighten when we count them.

—UNKNOWN

Daily Joys

Daily duties are daily joys, because they are something which God gives us to offer unto Him, to do our very best, in acknowledgment of His love.

—EDWARD BOUVERIE PUSEY

The Great Provider

Whether we are joyful or sad, God still remains faithful. He provides our needs, even if we don't get the lavish things we'd prefer. And He always provides generous spiritual blessings for those who trust in Him. No matter what your circumstances, you can always cling to Jesus—and be blessed.

Our work is meant to be a grace. It is a blessing and a gift, even a surprise and an act of unconditional love toward the community—and not just the present community that may or may not compensate us for our work, but the community to come, the generations that follow our work.

—MATTHEW FOX

So Small a Thing

It is so small a thing to have enjoyed
the sun, to have lived light in the spring,
to have loved, to have thought, to have done;
to have advanced true friends.

—M. ARNOLD

Celebrate!

"You will go out in joy and be led forth in peace; the mountains and hills will burst into song before you, and all the trees of the field will clap their hands. Instead of the thornbush will grow the pine tree, and instead of briers the myrtle will grow."

—ISAIAH 55:12–13 NIV

As Big as Life

Life without hope is an empty, boring,
and useless life. I cannot imagine that I could
strive for something if I did not carry hope in me.
I am thankful to God for this gift.
It is as big as life itself.

—VÁCLAV HAVEL

His Kiss of Peace

May God kiss you with His peace, as a father kisses his little child. And may you know that peace isn't a pot of gold rewarded to you after chasing some rainbow's end—it's a gift.

Always in Bloom

No matter what season of life you're in, you should bloom. Ask God to help you do the best you can. Ask Him to help you be a blessing wherever you are.

Unsung Heroes

The lives that have been the greatest blessing to you are the lives of those people who themselves were unaware of having been a blessing.

—OSWALD CHAMBERS

Give as Angels Give

Instead of a gem, or even a flower, we should cast the gift of a loving thought into the heart of a friend; that would be giving as the angels give.

—GEORGE MACDONALD

Christ gave each one of us the special gift of grace, showing how generous he is. That is why it says in the Scriptures, "When he went up to the heights, he led a parade of captives, and he gave gifts to people."

—EPHESIANS 4:7–8 NCV

Sharing Hearts

Over cups of tea, I listened to my friend, and my friend heard me. My joy was hers and hers was mine, as we shared our hearts line by line.

—UNKNOWN

Underestimated

The sun. . .in its full glory, either at rising or setting—this, and many other like blessings we enjoy daily; and for the most of them, because they are so common, most men forget to pay their praises. But let us not.

—IZAAK WALTON

Right Now

You don't have to be facing the end of your life to be blessed by Jesus. He wants to bless you today. He wants to shower many blessings on you for a lifetime, instead of limiting His impact to a few years.

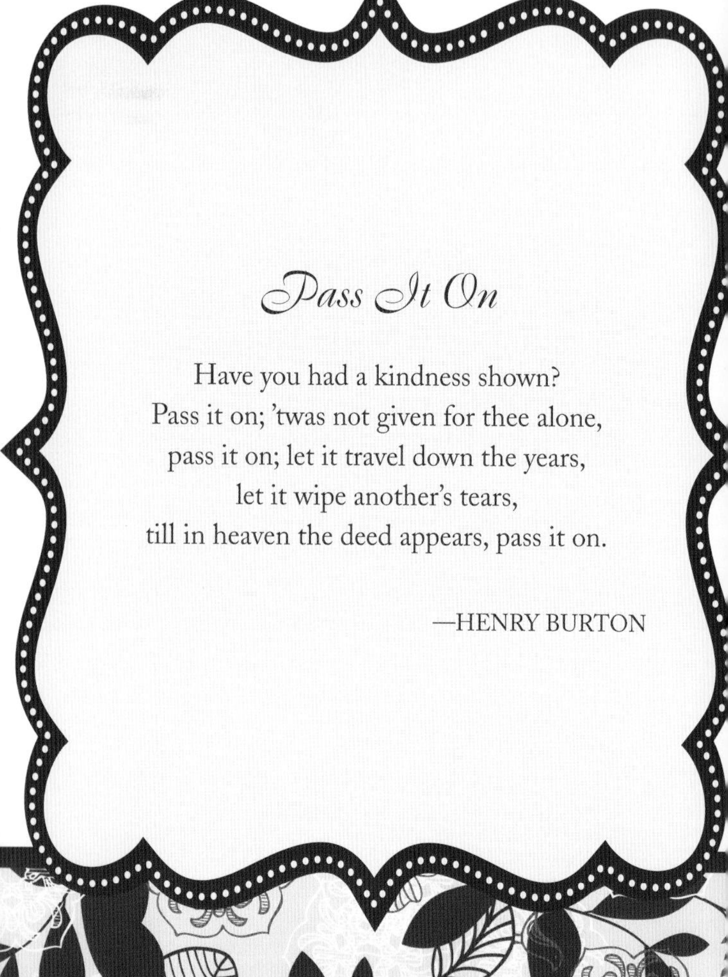

Pass It On

Have you had a kindness shown?
Pass it on; 'twas not given for thee alone,
pass it on; let it travel down the years,
let it wipe another's tears,
till in heaven the deed appears, pass it on.

—HENRY BURTON

A Never-Ending List

Heavenly Father, I have so much to be thankful for. My list of blessings is never-ending. May I never fail to praise You and to thank You for the many blessings You have given to me. Amen.

Shine

"You are the light that gives light to the world. A city that is built on a hill cannot be hidden. And people don't hide a light under a bowl. They put it on a lampstand so the light shines for all the people in the house. In the same way, you should be a light for other people. Live so that they will see the good things you do and will praise your Father in heaven."

—MATTHEW 5:14–16 NCV

Rest in Him

When God finds a soul that rests in Him and is not easily moved. . .He gives to such a soul the key to the treasures He has prepared for it so that it might enjoy them.

—CATHERINE OF GENOA

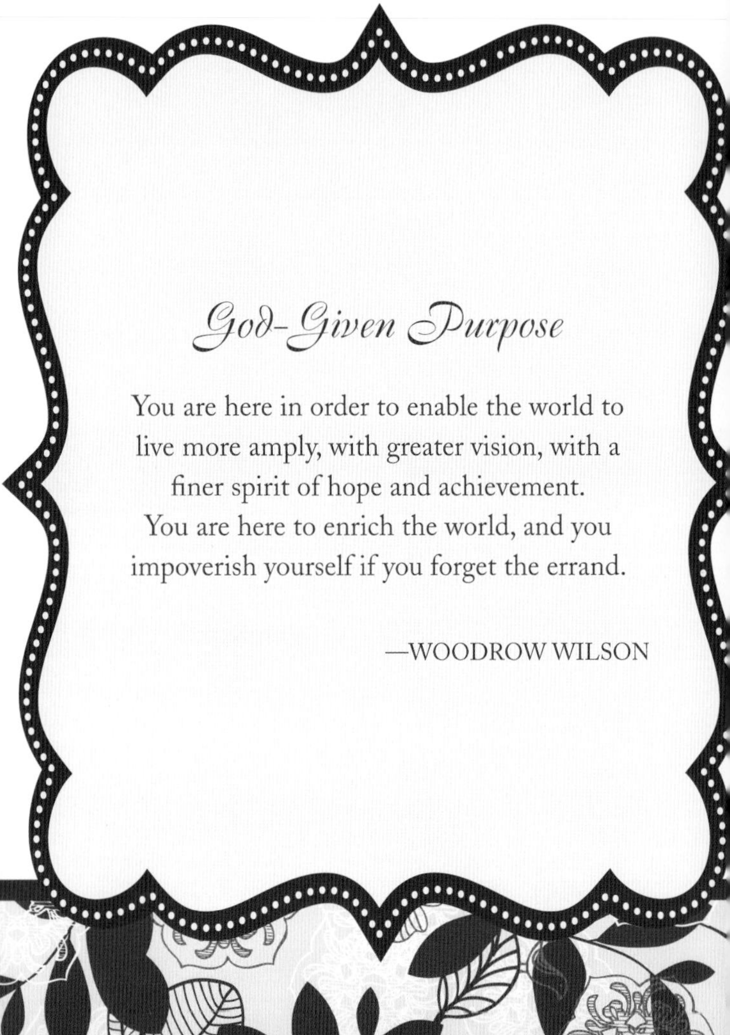

God-Given Purpose

You are here in order to enable the world to live more amply, with greater vision, with a finer spirit of hope and achievement. You are here to enrich the world, and you impoverish yourself if you forget the errand.

—WOODROW WILSON

God's Best Gift

No matter what gifts God gives us, we are to receive them with thanks. He made these gifts just for us, and we're enjoying the benefit, so why not share that joy with Jesus? He's the best gift God had to offer, the gift most to be received with thanksgiving.

The Golden Link

A mother's love is indeed the golden link that binds youth to age; and he is still but a child who can yet recall, with a softened heart, the fond devotion, or the gentle chidings of the best friend that God ever gave us.

—CHRISTIAN NESTELL BOVEE

God Is Everywhere

There's not a tint that paints the rose
Or decks the lily fair,
Or marks the humblest flower that grows,
But God has placed it there. . . .
There's not a place on earth's vast round,
In ocean's deep or air,
Where love and beauty are not found,
For God is everywhere.

—UNKNOWN

Delightful Blessings

Delight yourself in the Lord and he will
give you the desires of your heart.
Commit your way to the Lord; trust in
him and he will do this: He will make your
righteousness shine like the dawn, the justice of
your cause like the noonday sun.

—PSALM 37:4–6 NIV

Confidence Regained

Lord, help me to get over this nagging self-doubt. Remind me that Your blessings are forever and I have nothing to fear. Give me a merry heart, I pray.

The Key to Renewal

By reading the scriptures I am so renewed that all nature seems renewed around me and with me. The sky seems to be a pure, a cooler blue, the trees a deeper green. The whole world is charged with the glory of God, and I feel fire and music under my feet.

—THOMAS MERTON

God's Special Offer

This bright new day, complete with 24 hours of opportunities, choices, and attitudes comes with a perfectly matched set of 1,440 minutes. This unique gift, this one day, cannot be exchanged, replaced, or refunded. Handle with care. Make the most of it. There is only one per customer!

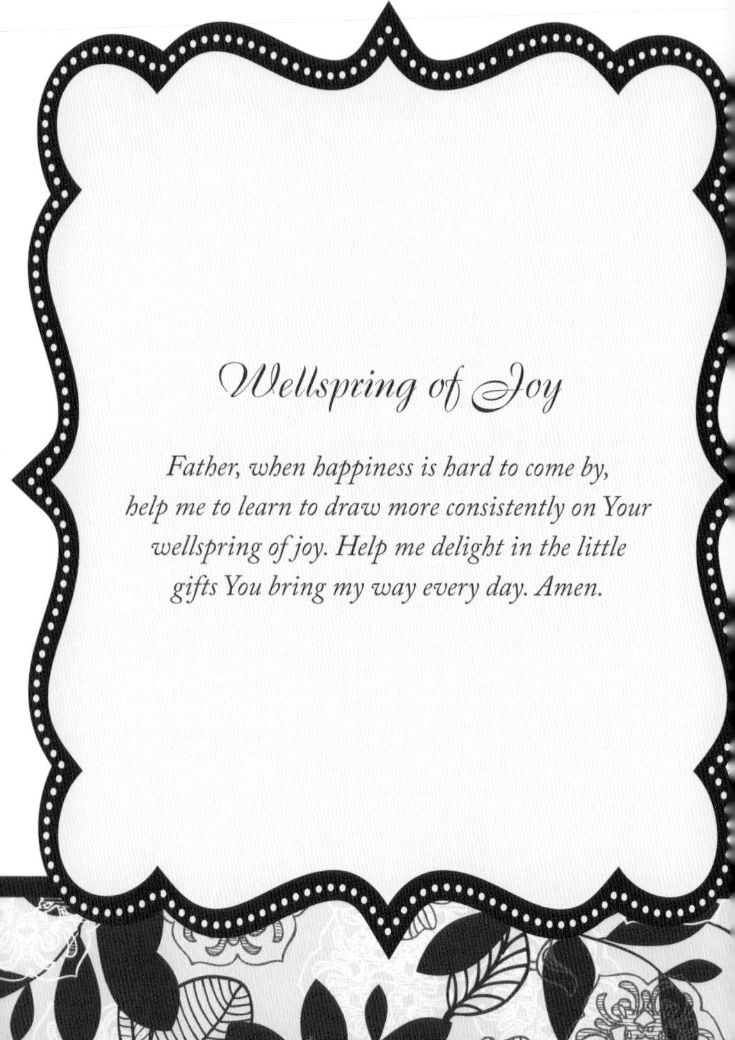

Wellspring of Joy

Father, when happiness is hard to come by, help me to learn to draw more consistently on Your wellspring of joy. Help me delight in the little gifts You bring my way every day. Amen.

Biblical Blessings

The Bible is one of the greatest blessings bestowed by God on the children of men. . . . It is all pure, all sincere; nothing too much; nothing wanting.

—JOHN LOCKE

Saving Love

"The Lord your God is with you, he is mighty to save. He will take great delight in you, he will quiet you with his love, he will rejoice over you with singing."

—ZEPHANIAH 3:17 NIV

Gratitude

Gratitude consists in a watchful, minute attention to the particulars of our state, and to the multitude of God's gifts, taken one by one. It fills us with a consciousness that God loves and cares for us, even to the least event and smallest need of life.

—HENRY EDWARD MANNING

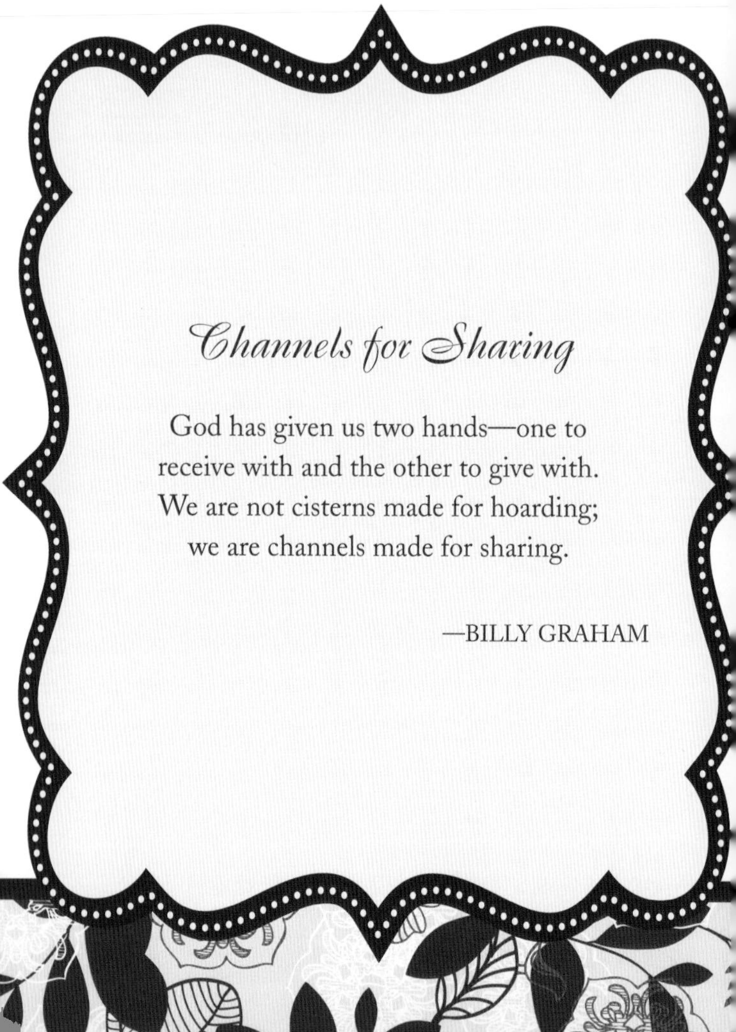

Channels for Sharing

God has given us two hands—one to receive with and the other to give with. We are not cisterns made for hoarding; we are channels made for sharing.

—BILLY GRAHAM

Perfect Timing

The moon marks off the seasons, and the
sun knows when to go down. . . . Then man
goes out to his work, to his labor until evening.
How many are your works, O Lord!
In wisdom you made them all.

—PSALM 104:19, 23–24 NIV

Be Glad

Be glad that your life has been full and complete,
Be glad that you've tasted the bitter and sweet.
Be glad that you've had such a full, happy life,
Be glad for your joy as well as your strife.
Be glad for the comfort that you've found in prayer.
Be glad for God's blessings, His love, and His care.

—HELEN STEINER RICE

Love Letters

The Bible is God's love letter to you. It isn't the sappy romance novel found in drugstores. . . . He is communicating His love to you. It's the love letter you've longed to read. Open it up and see for yourself.

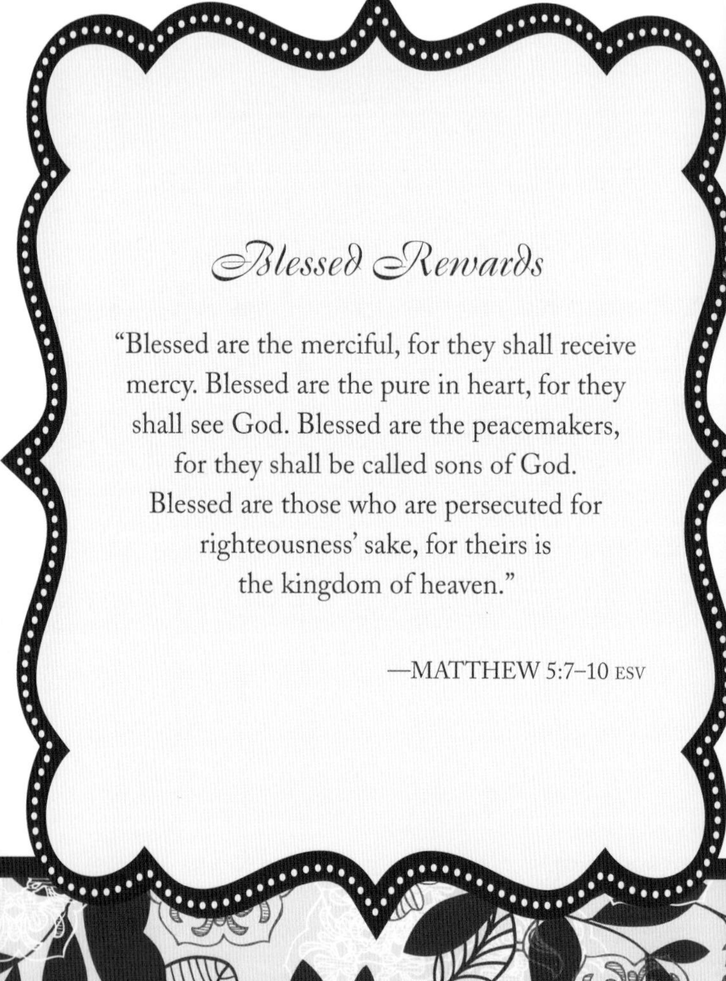

Blessed Rewards

"Blessed are the merciful, for they shall receive mercy. Blessed are the pure in heart, for they shall see God. Blessed are the peacemakers, for they shall be called sons of God. Blessed are those who are persecuted for righteousness' sake, for theirs is the kingdom of heaven."

—MATTHEW 5:7–10 ESV

The Kingdom on Earth

The kingdom of heaven and *The kingdom of God* are two phrases for the same thing. They mean not merely a future happy state in heaven, but a state to be enjoyed on earth.

Daily Reflection

The wonderful thing about sunset, and much the same can be said for sunrise, is that it happens every day, and even if the sunset itself is not spectacular, it marks the beginning of another day. It's a great time to pause and take notice.

—ELAINE ST. JAMES

Overwhelming Grace

Grace is such an overwhelming blessing that most of us dance around our understanding of it. We have a hard time understanding the completeness of it, the purity of it, the overwhelming comfort it offers. But, O Father, this is a gift, a promise like no other. It sets us free.

Precious Moments

Dear Lord, thank You for life's milestones that give us the opportunity to reflect on the bountiful gifts You've bestowed on us. May Your continued blessings be upon us as we celebrate each birthday, wedding, and funeral, always mindful of how precious each and every moment of our lives is. Amen.

Faith

Faith is the virtue by which, clinging to the faithfulness of God, we lean upon Him so that we may obtain what He gives us.

—WILLIAM AMES

His Masterpiece

We are God's masterpiece. He has created us anew in Christ Jesus, so we can do the good things he planned for us long ago.

—EPHESIANS 2:10 NLT

Father Knows Best

There's a country song called "Sometimes I Thank God for Unanswered Prayers." Its message is very powerful. What it is saying is that God knows what is best for us, and sometimes His answer to a prayer is no. Dear Lord, thank You for having the wisdom to know when to tell me no.

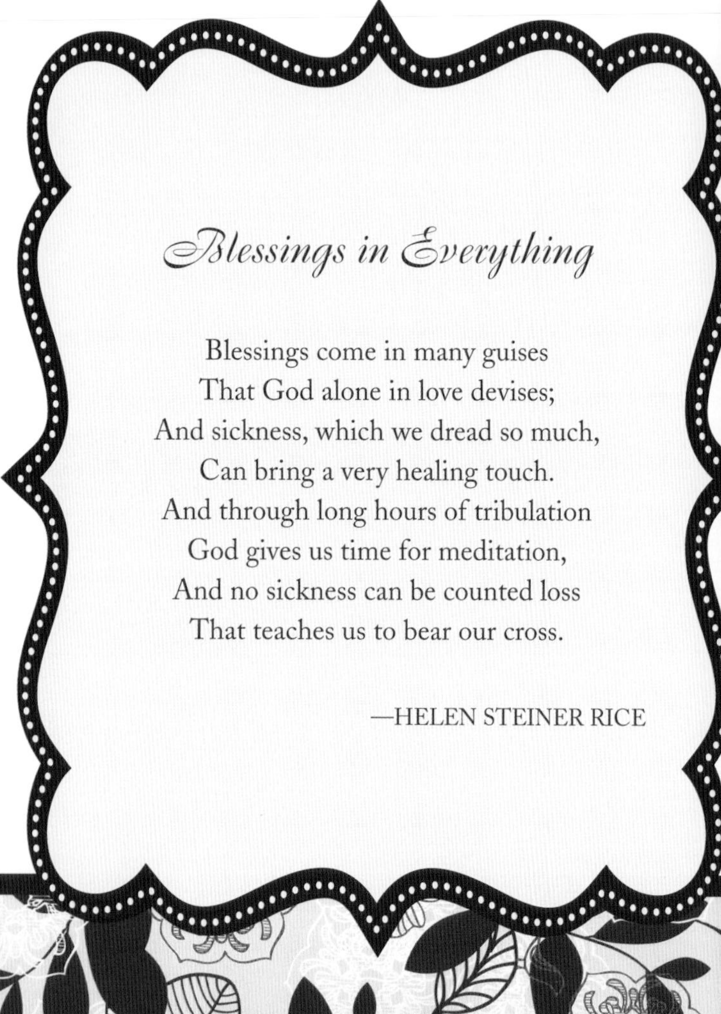

Blessings in Everything

Blessings come in many guises
That God alone in love devises;
And sickness, which we dread so much,
Can bring a very healing touch.
And through long hours of tribulation
God gives us time for meditation,
And no sickness can be counted loss
That teaches us to bear our cross.

—HELEN STEINER RICE

Memorable Footprints

Life is full of people who will make you laugh, cry, smile until your face hurts, and so happy that you think you'll burst. But the ones who leave their footprints on your soul are the ones that keep your life going.

—NATALIE BERNOT

Eager Anticipation

On that day when every tongue confesses that Jesus is Lord, we will experience the purest pleasure. Giving Jesus the glory on that day will be our greatest delight—one we look forward to with anticipation even now. We yearn for that glorious day.

Opportunities Everywhere

Embrace the wonder and excitement each day brings. For tomorrow affords us new opportunities. . .time to experience. . .time to create. . .time to reflect. . .time to dream.

—K. WILLIAMS

Abundant Showers

Rejoice in the Lord your God, for he has given you the autumn rains in righteousness. He sends you abundant showers, both autumn and spring rains, as before. The threshing floors will be filled with grain; the vats will overflow with new wine and oil.

—JOEL 2:23–24 NIV

Praise Him!

For the invasion of my soul by Thy Holy Spirit: for all human love and goodness that speaks to me of Thee: for the fullness of Thy glory outpoured in Jesus Christ, I give Thee thanks, O God.

—JOHN BAILLIE

Unchangeable Beauty

The beauty of the earth, the beauty of the sky,
the order of the stars, the sun, the moon. . .
their very loveliness is their confession of God:
For who made these lovely mutable things,
but He who is Himself unchangeable beauty?

—ST. AUGUSTINE

Our Personal Storehouse

Memories are very private things,
a personal storehouse of treasures and sorrows.
What a gift God gave us when He created our
brains with the ability to remember!

Go with Purpose

We may run, walk, stumble. . .or fly, but let us never lose sight of the reason for the journey or miss a chance to see a rainbow on the way.

—GLORIA GAITHER

Our Friend, Jesus

The Creator thinks enough of you to have sent Someone very special so that you might have life—abundantly, joyfully, completely, and victoriously.

Promise of Home

In my Father's house are many mansions: if it were not so, I would have told you. I go to prepare a place for you. And if I go and prepare a place for you, I will come again, and receive you unto myself; that where I am, there ye may be also.

—JOHN 14:2–3 KJV

Don't Despair!

Refuse to be discouraged,
refuse to be distressed,
For when we are despondent,
our lives cannot be blessed.
For doubt and fear and worry
close the door to faith and prayer,
And there's no room for blessings
when we're lost in deep despair.
But when we view our problems
through the eyes of God above,
Misfortunes turn to blessings
and hatred turns to love.

—HELEN STEINER RICE

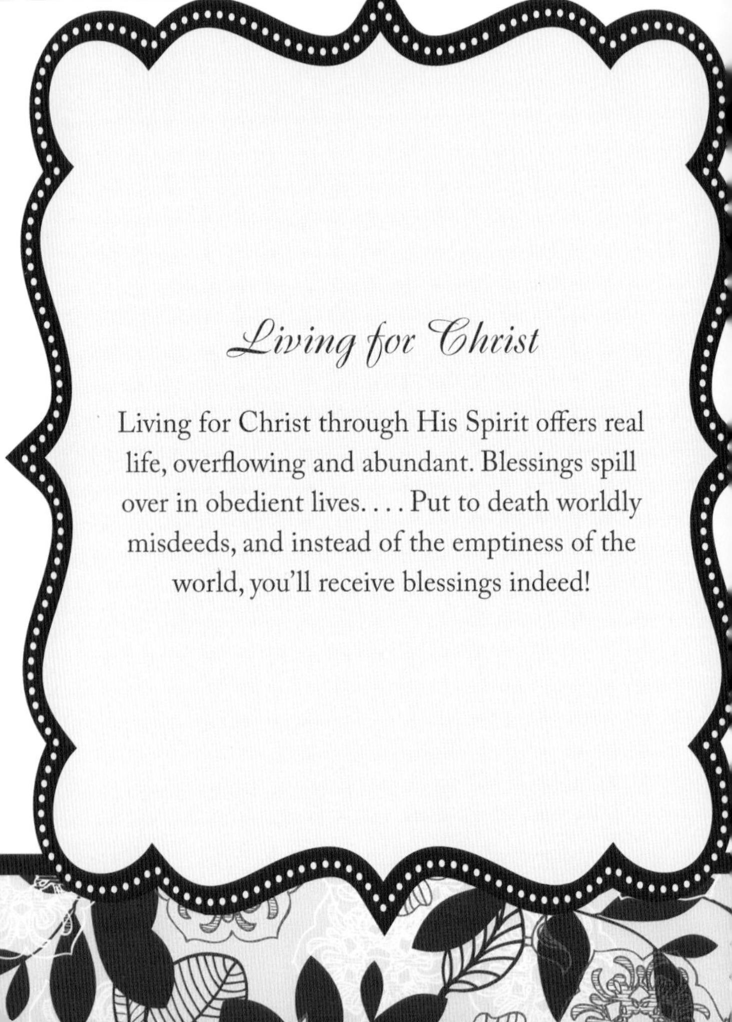

Living for Christ

Living for Christ through His Spirit offers real life, overflowing and abundant. Blessings spill over in obedient lives. . . . Put to death worldly misdeeds, and instead of the emptiness of the world, you'll receive blessings indeed!

Recognition

God recognizes that we have received His forgiveness, through His Son, and He's happy to grant us our wishes. He gives good things that make us happy. That doesn't mean He gives us everything we ask for. But when we ask in Jesus' will, God is happy to give.

He Will Provide

God wants nothing from us except our needs, and these furnish Him with room to display His bounty when He supplies them freely. . . . Not what I have, but what I do not have, is the first point of contact between my soul and God.

—CHARLES SPURGEON

Strong Friendships

Life is a chronicle of friendship.
Friends create a world anew each day.
Without their loving care, courage would
not suffice to keep hearts strong for life.

—HELEN KELLER

Peaceful Sleep

It is vain for you to rise up early,
to sit up late, to eat the bread of sorrows;
for so He gives His beloved sleep.

—PSALM 127:2 NKJV

Morning Prayer

Dear Lord, thank You for another new day. Help me taste the richness of the coffee in my cup and prepare me to recognize Your bountiful blessings in unexpected places. Remind me not to take these tiny treasures for granted. Give me a child's heart that sees the lovely simple things in life. Amen.

Sweet Surprises

Into our lives come many things
to break the dull routine—
The things we had not planned on
that happen unforeseen:
The unexpected little joys that
are scattered on our way,
Success we did not count on
or a rare, fulfilling day,
And every lucky happening and every lucky break
Are little gifts from God above that
are ours to freely take.

—HELEN STEINER RICE

Unexpected Gifts

A much-needed gift received at the perfect moment is always welcome, even if it comes at no special holiday. God knows that—and understands the importance of timing for everything He gives. . . . His presents are always timely, always perfect, and are certain to be received with thanks by a heart that's truly His.

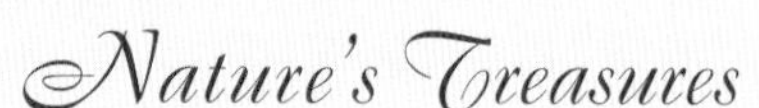

Nature's Treasures

If we are children of God, we have a tremendous treasure in nature and will realize that it is holy and sacred. We will see God reaching out to us in every wind that blows, every sunrise and sunset, every cloud in the sky, every flower that blooms, and every leaf that fades.

—OSWALD CHAMBERS

Daily Nourishment

Family life is full of major and minor crises—the ups and downs of health, success and failure in careers, marriage, and divorce—and all kinds of characters. With all of these felt details, life etches itself into memory and personality. It's difficult to imagine anything more nourishing to the soul.

—THOMAS MOORE

Lavish Blessings

How great is the goodness you have stored up for those who fear you. You lavish it on those who come to you for protection, blessing them before the watching world.

—PSALM 31:19 NLT

Grace and Peace

As you look around at God's blessings in your life, close your eyes and look inward as well. God has also provided you with an abundance of grace and peace. Grace that allows you to be who you genuinely are and the peace of knowing that who you are is just fine with Him.

Get Happy!

We act as though comfort and luxury were the chief requirements in life, when all we need to make us really happy is something to be enthusiastic about.

—CHARLES KINGSLEY

Are You Ready?

God wants to bless you, and He will, but perhaps He has to get your attention first. As long as you're headed in the opposite direction, even if you received a blessing, you wouldn't appreciate it. Even the best God could give would become mired in your disobedience. God wants to bless you today. Are you ready to receive all the good He has to offer?

God's Grace

We know certainly that our God. . .gives us every grace, every abundant grace; and though we are so weak of ourselves, this grace is able to carry us through every obstacle and difficulty.

—ELIZABETH ANN SETON

Wise Requests

Give me work to do; give me health; give me joy in simple things. Give me an eye for beauty, a tongue for truth, a heart that loves, and at the close of each day give me a book, and a friend with whom I can be silent.

Between His Shoulders

"Let the beloved of the Lord rest secure in him, for he shields him all day long, and the one the Lord loves rests between his shoulders". . . . "May the Lord bless his land with the precious dew from heaven above and with the deep waters that lie below; with the best the sun brings forth and the finest the moon can yield."

—DEUTERONOMY 33:12–14 NIV

Possibilities Blessings

No matter how dark things seem to be or actually are, raise your sights and see possibilities—always see them, for they're always there.

—NORMAN VINCENT PEALE

Patient Revelations

Our real blessings often appear to us in the shape of pains, losses, and disappointments; but let us have patience and we soon shall see them in their proper figures.

—JOSEPH ADDISON

The Best Road Map

God left us an owner's manual—the Bible. It's a road map for life. In it, you'll discover the paths that lead to health, wholeness, peace, renewed strength, and a beautiful life.

Sing an Angel's Song

Kind words are the music of the world. They have a power which seems to be beyond natural causes, as if they were some angel's song which had lost its way and come on earth.

—FREDERICK WILLIAM FABER

The Privilege of Prayer

What a friend we have in Jesus,
All our sins and griefs to bear.
What a privilege to carry
Everything to God in prayer.

—JOSEPH SCRIVEN

Infinitely Blessed

"And all these blessings shall come upon you and
overtake you, because you obey the voice of the
Lord your God: Blessed shall you be in the city,
and blessed shall you be in the country. . . .
Blessed shall you be when you come in,
and blessed shall you be when you go out."

—DEUTERONOMY 28:2–3, 6 NKJV

The Happiest Moments

The happiest moments of my life
have been the few which I have passed
at home in the bosom of my family.

—THOMAS JEFFERSON

Size Doesn't Matter

If you have a special need today, focus your full attention on the goodness and greatness of your Father rather than on the size of your need. Your need is so small compared to His ability to meet it.

Happy Coincidences

Dear Lord, thank You for happy coincidences and days when things just seem to fall into place. Help me to always remember and recognize these moments as examples of Your awesome power working in my life. All credit goes to You for the good things that come my way. Amen.

Salvation

The gift of God is that you have been saved through faith. Neither this faith nor salvation is owing to any works you ever did, will, or can do.

Use Your Gifts

Whosoever takes up the burden of his neighbor. . .and ministers unto those in need out of the abundance of things he has received. . .of God's bounty—this man. . . is an imitator of God.

—DIOGNETUS

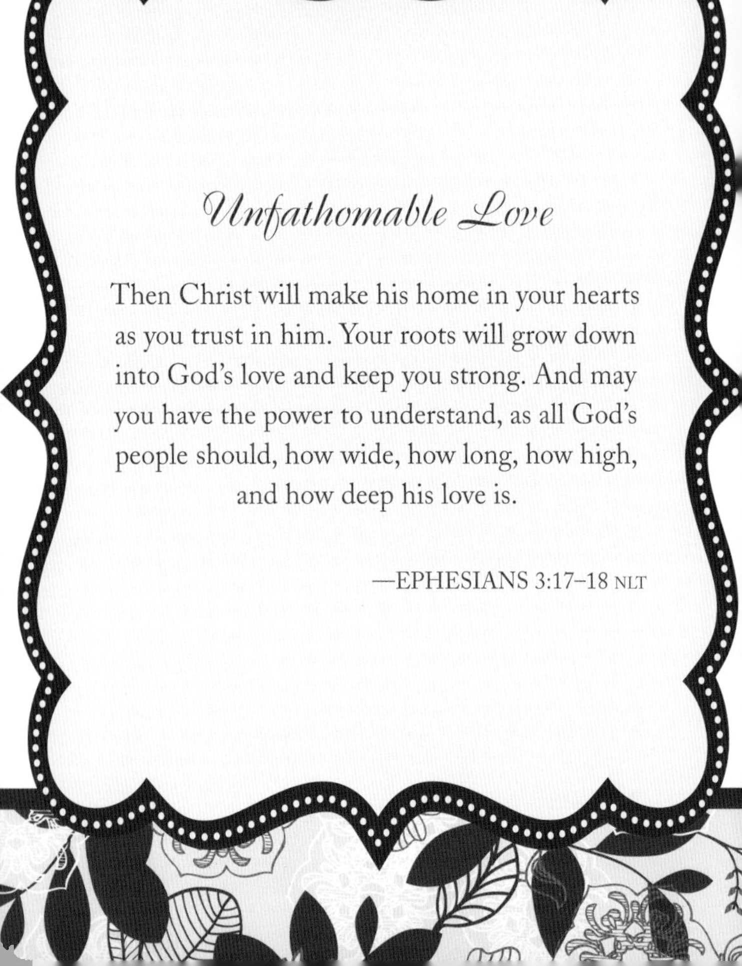

Unfathomable Love

Then Christ will make his home in your hearts as you trust in him. Your roots will grow down into God's love and keep you strong. And may you have the power to understand, as all God's people should, how wide, how long, how high, and how deep his love is.

—EPHESIANS 3:17–18 NLT

Home Sweet Home

O Thou, who dwellest in so many homes, possess Thyself of this. Bless the life that is sheltered here. Grant that trust and peace and comfort abide within, and that love and life and usefulness may go out from this home forever.

—UNKNOWN

Hidden Ideals

God hides some ideal in every human soul.
At some time in our life we feel a trembling,
fearful longing to do some good thing.
Life finds its noblest spring of excellence in
this hidden impulse to do our best.

—ROBERT COLLYER

Spontaneous Blessings

Some of the best things in your life will come to you because of planning. But some. . .will also come without planning for them at all. That's what makes life so much fun. It's a daily surprise, and you need to stride into it with faith, even if you don't know where you're going.

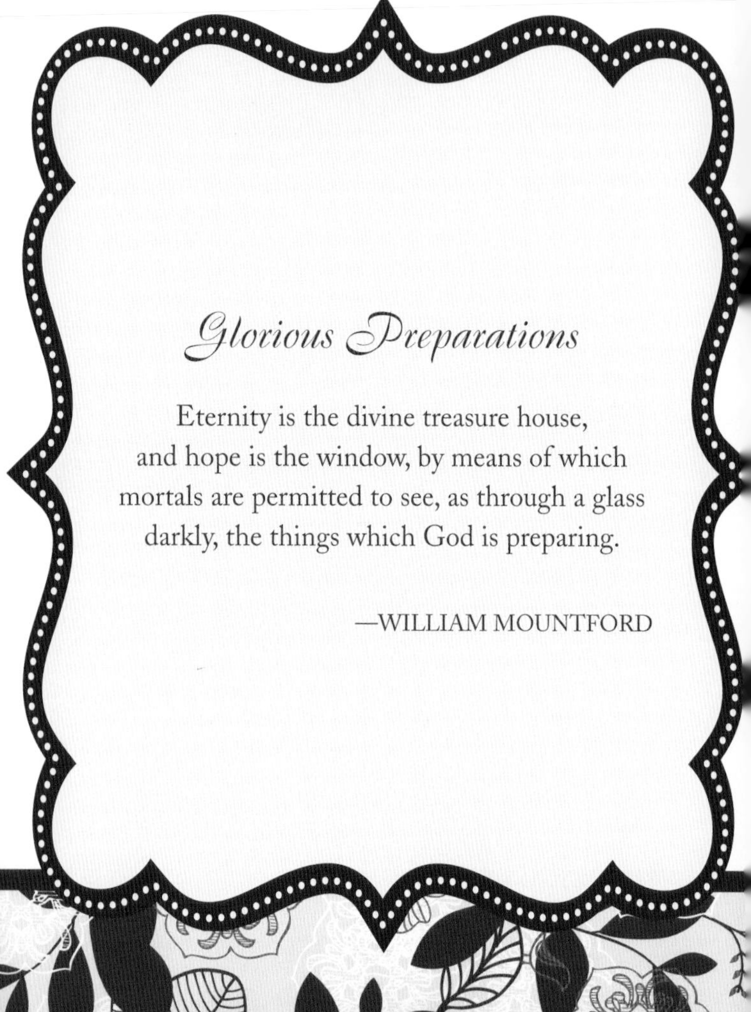

Glorious Preparations

Eternity is the divine treasure house,
and hope is the window, by means of which
mortals are permitted to see, as through a glass
darkly, the things which God is preparing.

—WILLIAM MOUNTFORD

Seeds of Peace

Lord, thank You for blessing me with so many fruitful relationships. Even when I'm feeling down or stuck in a rut, You've always led me to a helping hand or an understanding shoulder to cry on. Thank You for cultivating a sense of joy in me when I'm around those I love. I ask that You'd use me to spread Your seeds of peace in their lives as well. Amen.

The Best Gift-Giver

"If you then, being evil, know how to give good gifts to your children, how much more will your Father who is in heaven give good things to those who ask Him!"

—MATTHEW 7:11 NKJV

Adversity Begets Blessings

If we had no winter, the spring would not be so pleasant: If we did not sometimes taste of adversity, prosperity would not be so welcome.

—ANNE BRADSTREET

Ordinary things have a great power to reveal the mysterious nearness of a caring, liberating God. . . . In what seems ordinary and everyday there is always more than at first meets the eye.

—CHARLES CUMMINGS

More Than We Consider

Our heavenly Father knows how to give the best—gifts that have no price. A sunset filled with vibrant colors, a nighttime sky. . .sprinkled with glowing stars, a drink of water that quenches thirst as no manmade beverage can. God has given generously, in many more ways than we often consider.

Many Guises

When troubles come and things go wrong
And days are cheerless and nights are long,
We add to our worries by refusing to try
To look for the rainbow in an overcast sky. . .
Not knowing God sent it not to distress us
But to strengthen our faith and
redeem us and bless us.

—HELEN STEINER RICE

Thankfulness Remains

First among the things to be thankful for is a thankful spirit. . . . Happy are they who possess this gift! Blessings may fail and fortunes vary, but the thankful heart remains.

—UNKNOWN

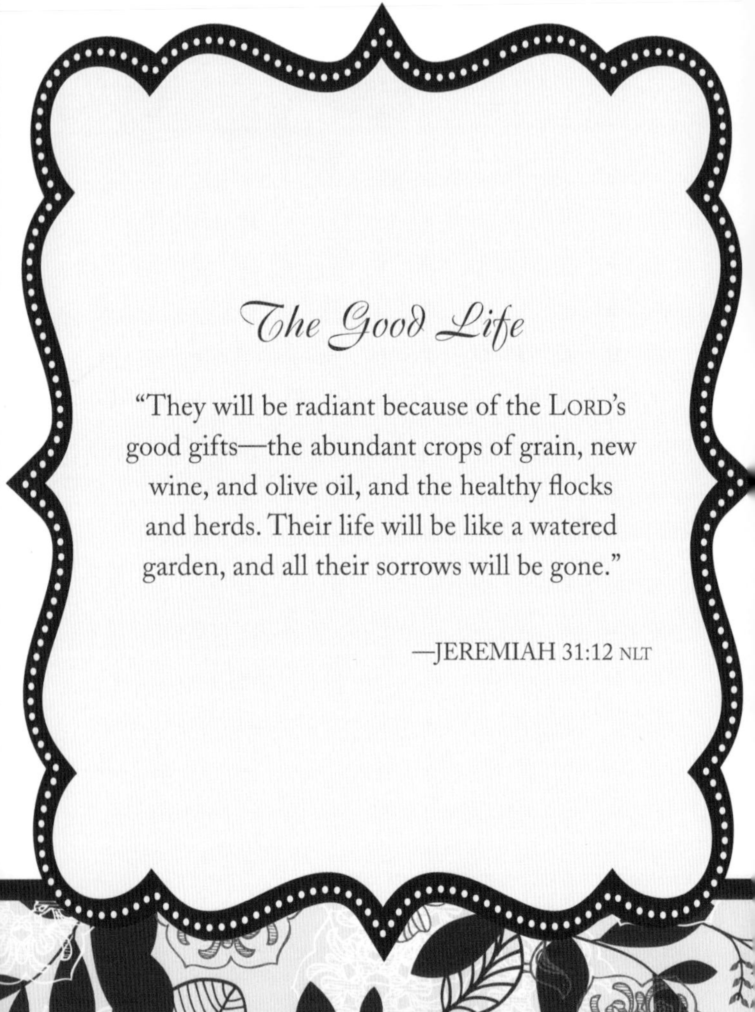

The Good Life

"They will be radiant because of the Lord's good gifts—the abundant crops of grain, new wine, and olive oil, and the healthy flocks and herds. Their life will be like a watered garden, and all their sorrows will be gone."

—JEREMIAH 31:12 NLT

Reap in Abundance

The world is sown with good; but unless I turn my glad thoughts into practical living and till my own field, I cannot reap a kernel of good.

—HELEN KELLER

The Choice Is Yours

Between the house and the store there are little pockets of happiness. A bird, a garden, a friend's greeting, a child's smile, a cat in the sunshine needing a stroke. Recognize them or ignore them. It's always up to you.

—PAM BROWN

Heavenly Treasures

Even the poorest people on earth can lay aside eternal blessings. That's because heavenly treasures have nothing to do with our legal tender—no government creates or backs it. God's riches are collected in a currency of the heart that consists of things like forgiveness, humility, and charitable deeds.

I will take special notice of the good things when they come. I will fix my mind on what is pure and lovely and upright. . . . I will not worry but keep on producing a life that is a blessing for You and others. Let me take time often to come drink from Your quiet stream. I thank You for it.

—ANITA CORRINE DONIHUE

Forever Grateful

The private and personal blessings we enjoy, the blessings of immunity, safeguard, liberty, and integrity, deserve the thanksgiving of a whole life.

—JEREMY TAYLOR

Our Reward

This is what I have seen to be good and right: to eat and drink and be happy in all the work one does under the sun during the few years of his life which God has given him. For this is his pay. . . . This is the gift of God.

—ECCLESIASTES 5:18–19 NLV

Sweet Gratitude

As flowers carry dewdrops, trembling on the edges of the petals, and ready to fall at the first waft of the wind or brush of bird, so the heart should carry its beaded words of thanksgiving. At the first breath of heavenly flavor, let down the shower, perfumed with the heart's gratitude.

—HENRY WARD BEECHER

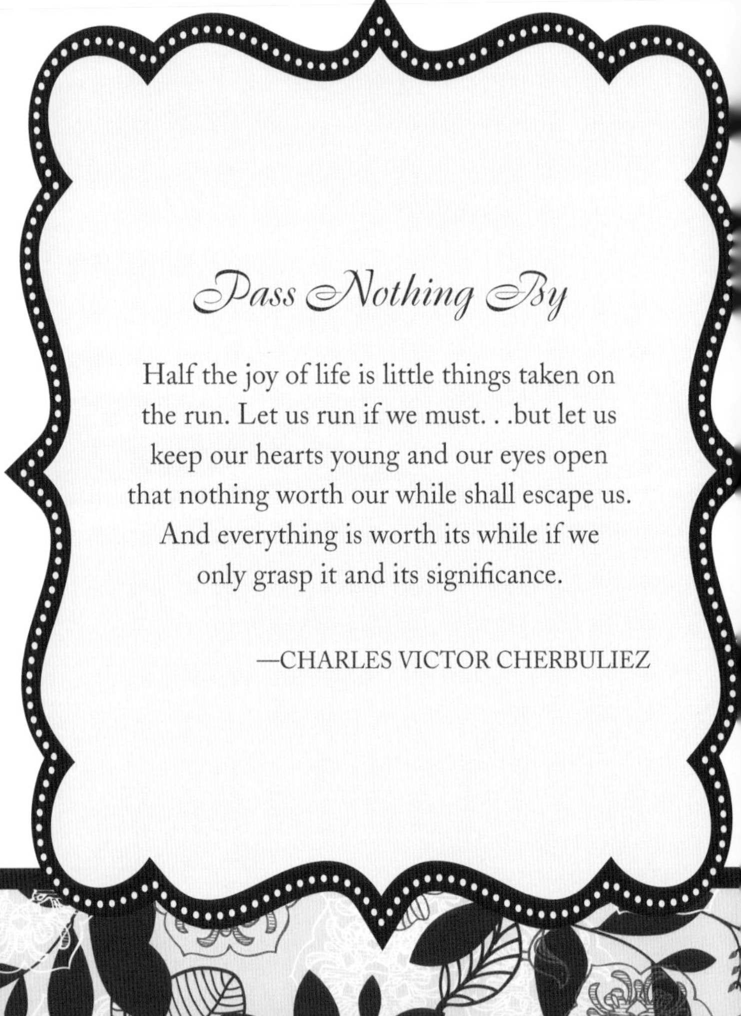

Pass Nothing By

Half the joy of life is little things taken on the run. Let us run if we must. . .but let us keep our hearts young and our eyes open that nothing worth our while shall escape us. And everything is worth its while if we only grasp it and its significance.

—CHARLES VICTOR CHERBULIEZ

A Little Effort, Big Rewards

Sometimes God doesn't hand us our rewards—we have to find them. It's not that God is playing games with us. He just knows that a little effort on our part will make us appreciate our rewards all the more.

Give Thanks for Diversity

Appreciate the members of your family for who they are, even though their outlook or style may be miles different from yours. Rabbits don't fly. Eagles don't swim. Ducks look funny trying to climb. Squirrels don't have feathers. Stop comparing. There's plenty of room in the forest.

—CHUCK SWINDOLL

The Sweetest Joy

Friendship is one of the sweetest joys of life. Many might have failed beneath the bitterness of their trial had they not found a friend.

—CHARLES SPURGEON

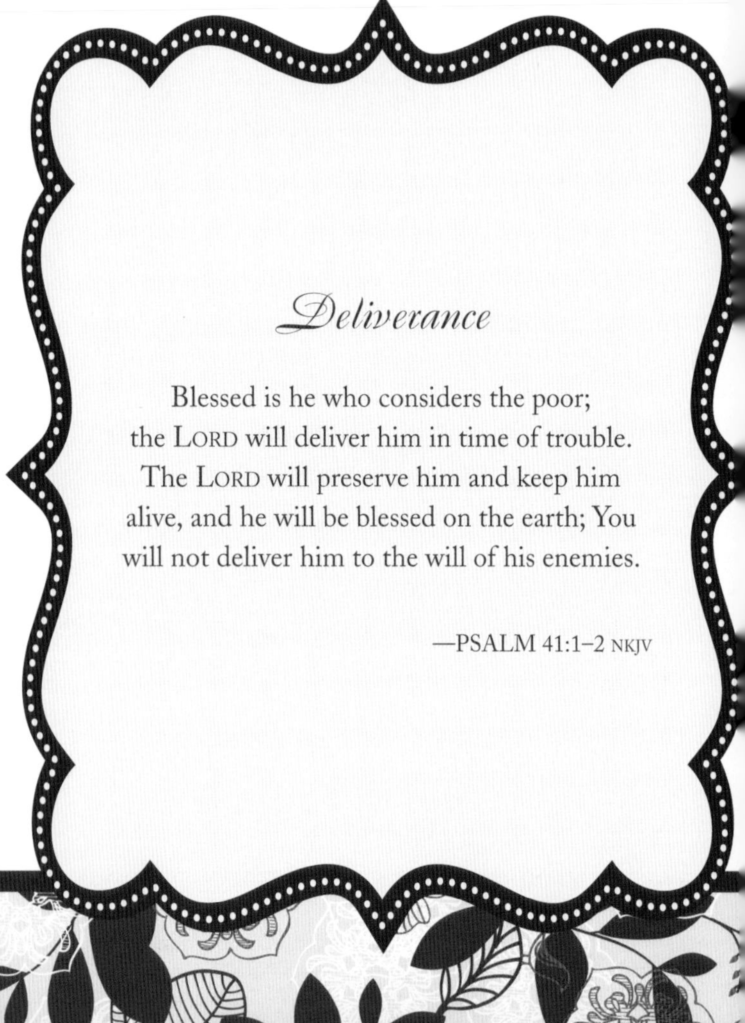

Deliverance

Blessed is he who considers the poor;
the Lord will deliver him in time of trouble.
The Lord will preserve him and keep him
alive, and he will be blessed on the earth; You
will not deliver him to the will of his enemies.

—PSALM 41:1–2 NKJV

Go Forward Joyously

A new life begins for us with every second.
Let us go forward joyously to meet it.
We must press on, whether we will or no,
and we shall walk better with our eyes
before us than with them ever cast behind.

—UNKNOWN

Gentle Guidance

Father, I know You will provide what's best for me, even if I don't understand at the time. Let me walk in faith, confident that You know my path better than I do. Amen.

Personalized Gifts

God gives each of us different lives and different blessings, designed just for us. Those blessings provide goodness and mercy on earth and continued joy in heaven. There's no dissonance between our song here on earth and the one that will praise Jesus eternally.

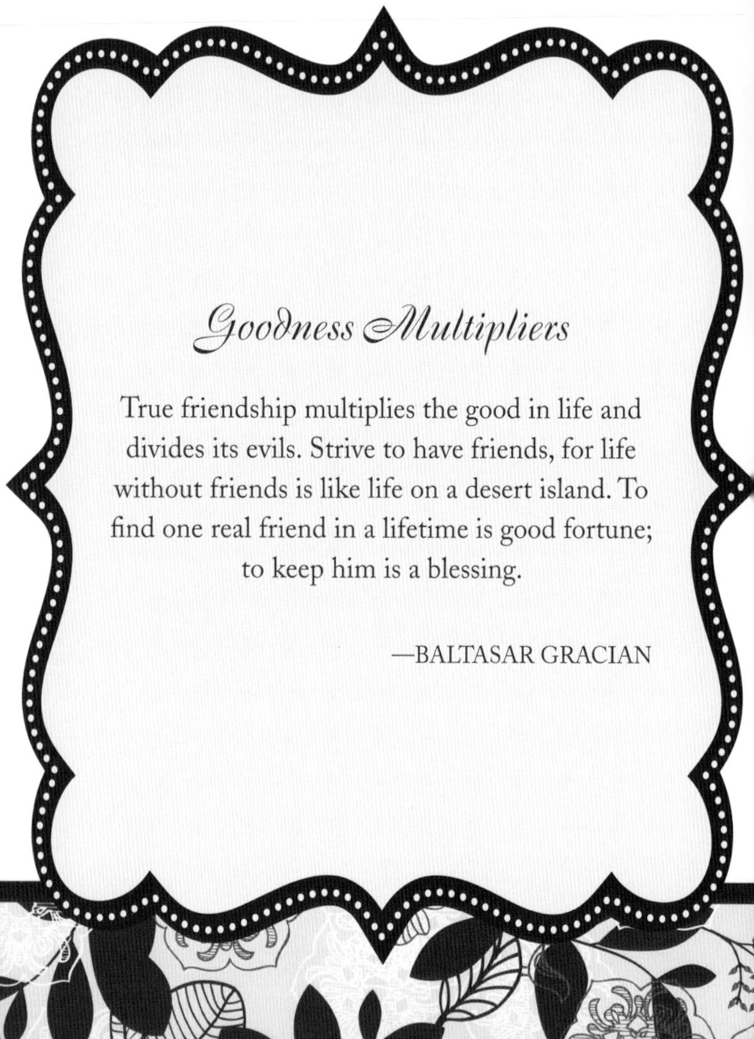

Goodness Multipliers

True friendship multiplies the good in life and divides its evils. Strive to have friends, for life without friends is like life on a desert island. To find one real friend in a lifetime is good fortune; to keep him is a blessing.

—BALTASAR GRACIAN

Satisfaction

Sometimes your expectation for the blessings of God requires you to press a little harder and stretch your faith a little further to see the results you've asked God for. You can be sure all your effort will be rewarded.

Our Watchful Keeper

For sunlit hours and visions clear,
For all remembered faces dear. . .
For friends who shared the year's long road,
And bore with us the common load. . .
For insights won through toil and tears,
We thank the Keeper of our years.

—CLYDE MCGEE

Be a Blessing

Everyone you meet is fighting some kind of battle, and your smile, your kind word, your hand of friendship will make a difference in their day and will change how they see things. You can be the change. You can bless those around you.

—KAREN MOORE

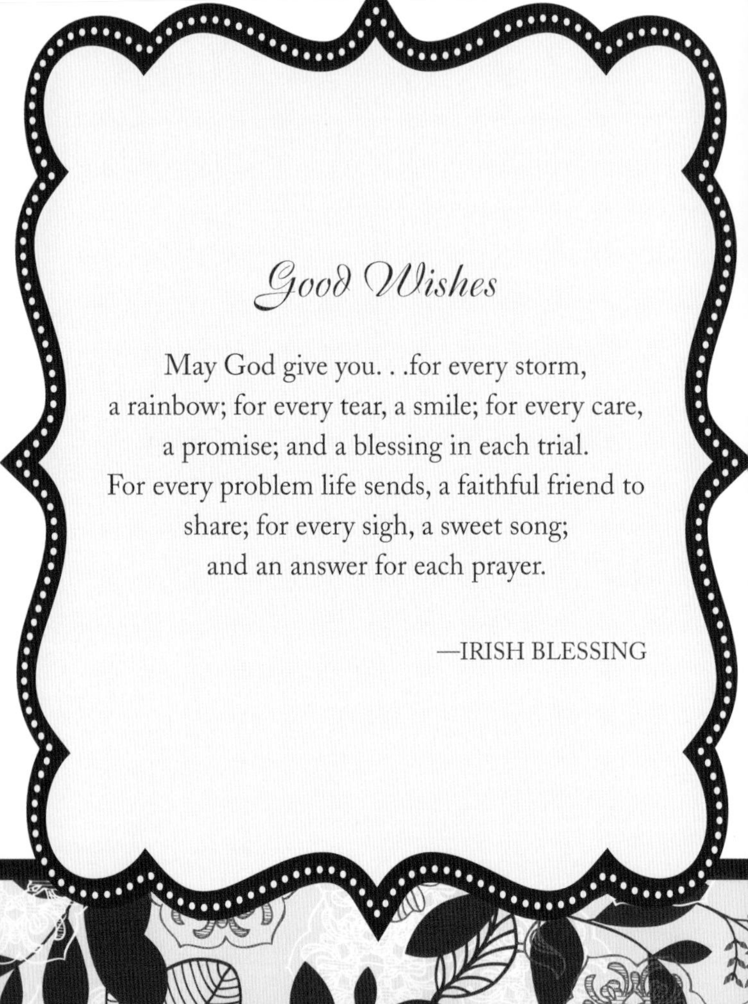

Good Wishes

May God give you. . .for every storm,
a rainbow; for every tear, a smile; for every care,
a promise; and a blessing in each trial.
For every problem life sends, a faithful friend to
share; for every sigh, a sweet song;
and an answer for each prayer.

—IRISH BLESSING

Share the News!

God has wonderful gifts in mind for you. If you ask, He'll show you what gifts He's given you and how He wants you to impact others with them. Don't wait until eternity to experience the joys and delights of faith—share some of that good news today!

Two Ways to Live

There are only two ways to live your life.
One is as though nothing is a miracle.
The other is as though everything is a miracle.

—ALBERT EINSTEIN

Hidden Rewards

*O Lord, You care for every part of my life and
know me inside out. Although some of my
rewards may be hidden right now,
I am confident You will help me find them. Amen.*

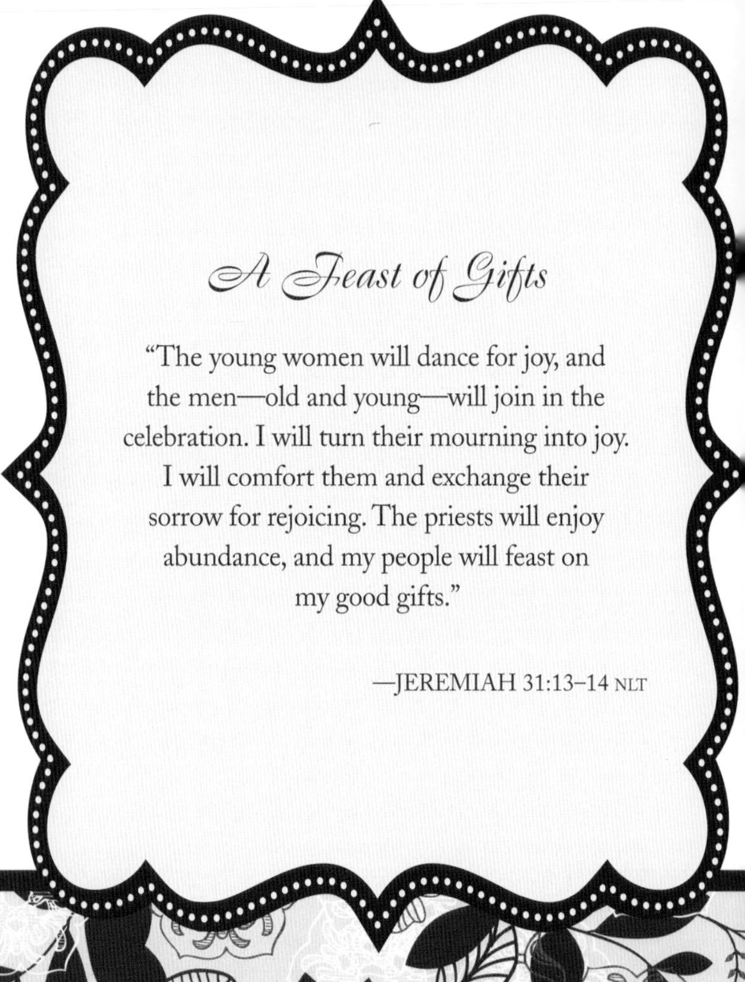

A Feast of Gifts

"The young women will dance for joy, and
the men—old and young—will join in the
celebration. I will turn their mourning into joy.
I will comfort them and exchange their
sorrow for rejoicing. The priests will enjoy
abundance, and my people will feast on
my good gifts."

—JEREMIAH 31:13–14 NLT

Miracles

To be alive, to be able to see, to walk, to have a home. . .friends—it's all a miracle. I have adopted the technique of living life from miracle to miracle.

—ARTHUR RUBENSTEIN

God's Keeping

To be in God's keeping is surely a blessing,
For though life is often dark and distressing,
No day is too dark and no burden too great
That God in His love cannot penetrate.

—HELEN STEINER RICE

Joyous Sounds

May none of God's wonderful works keep silence,
night or morning. Bright stars, high mountains,
the depths of the seas, sources of rushing rivers:
May all these break into song as we sing to
the Father, Son, and Holy Spirit.

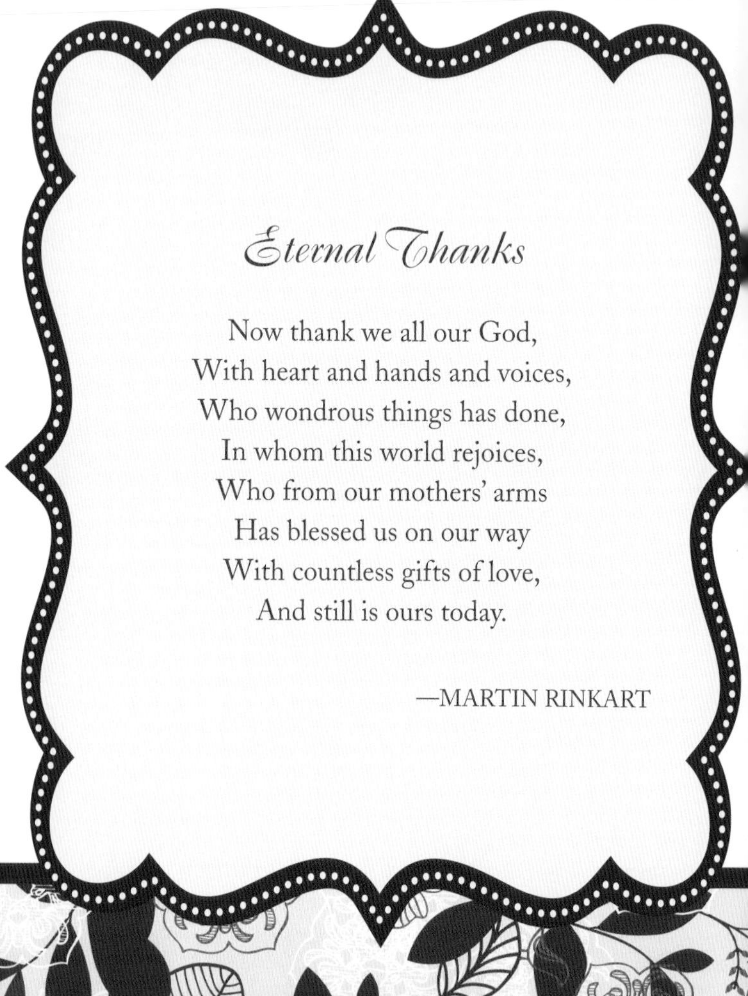

Eternal Thanks

Now thank we all our God,
With heart and hands and voices,
Who wondrous things has done,
In whom this world rejoices,
Who from our mothers' arms
Has blessed us on our way
With countless gifts of love,
And still is ours today.

—MARTIN RINKART

True Contentment

We tend to forget that happiness doesn't come as a result of getting something we don't have, but rather of recognizing and appreciating what we do have.

—FREDERICK KOENIG

Holiday Gifts

You have made known to me the path of life;
you will fill me with joy in your presence,
with eternal pleasures at your right hand.

—PSALM 16:11 NIV

The Miracle of Kindness

This is the miracle that happens every time to those who really love; the more they give, the more they possess.

—RAINER MARIA RILKE

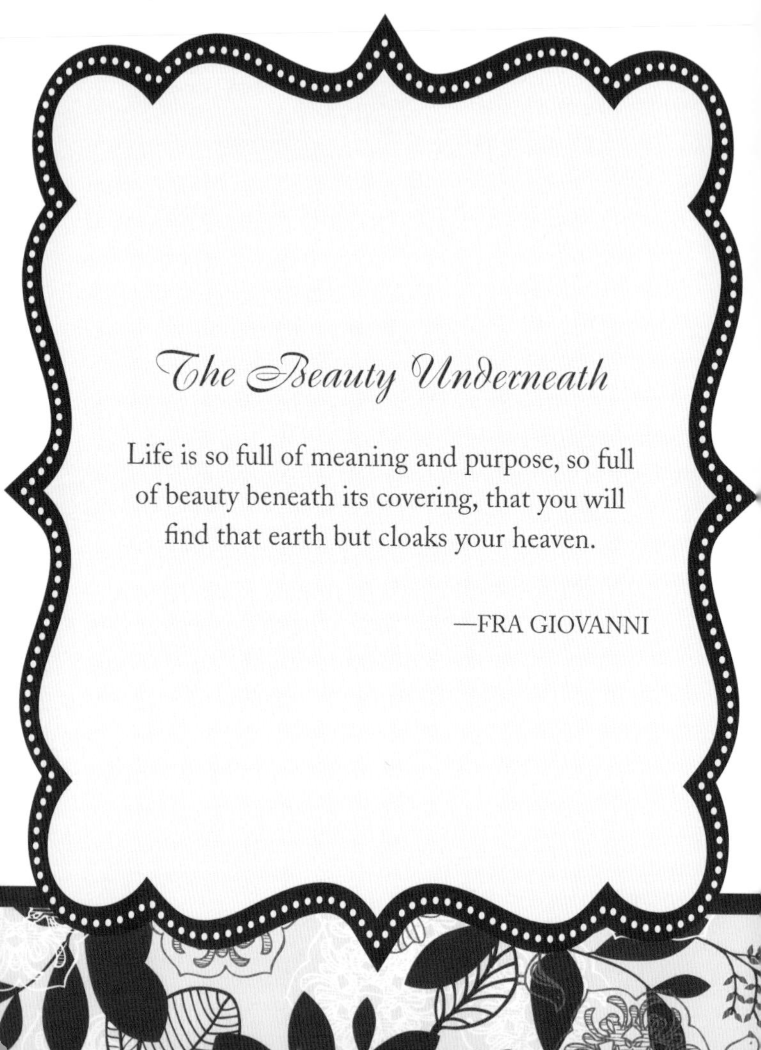

The Beauty Underneath

Life is so full of meaning and purpose, so full of beauty beneath its covering, that you will find that earth but cloaks your heaven.

—FRA GIOVANNI

Spiritual Fill-Up

What a blessing, to continually receive more and more of God's mercy, peace, and love. God gives blessings so we can encourage, teach, and lead others into a relationship with Him. If we receive God's gifts and pass them on to others, God fills us again.

Daily Treasures

Dear Jesus, help me not to be so busy that I miss the small pleasures You've sprinkled through my day. Help me notice the way the sunlight flickers through the leaves outside my kitchen window; help me pay attention to the smile of sympathy my coworker gives me. I thank You for all Your gifts, seen and unseen. Amen.

—ELLYN SANNA

Quiet Blessings

How silently, how silently the wondrous gift is given. So God imparts to human hearts the wonders of His heaven.

—PHILLIPS BROOKS

The Ultimate Gift

But when the right time came, God sent
his Son, born of a woman, subject to the law.
God sent him to buy freedom for us who were
slaves to the law, so that he could adopt
us as his very own children.

—GALATIANS 4:4–5 NLT

A Reason to Rejoice

'Twas a humble birthplace, but O how much God gave to us that day, from the manger bed what a path has led, what a perfect, holy way. Alleluia! O how the angels sang. Alleluia! How it rang! And the sky was bright with a holy light—'twas the birthday of a King.

—WILLIAM H. NEIDLINGER

Whatever Is Best

And always, God's ready and eager and willing
To pour out His mercy, completely fulfilling:
All of man's needs for peace, joy, and rest,
For God gives His children whatever is best.
Just give Him the chance to open His treasures,
And He'll fill your life with unfathomable pleasures.

—HELEN STEINER RICE

Give and Receive

God offers this wonderful blessing: Those who give will also receive. Whether it's money, time, energy, or another commodity, spiritual or physical, God does not forget anything we've done. He never ignores any generous gifts we offer at a price to ourselves.

Under His Wing

Look back through all of your experiences and think of the ways that the Lord your God has led you and how He has fed and clothed you every day.

A Limitless Supply

You can trust God right now to supply all your needs for today. And if your needs are more tomorrow, His supply will be greater also.

—UNKNOWN

Unwavering Faith

We are ignored, even though we are well known.
We live close to death, but we are still alive.
We have been beaten, but we have not been killed.
Our hearts ache, but we always have joy.
We are poor, but we give spiritual riches to others.
We own nothing, and yet we have everything.

—2 CORINTHIANS 6:9–10 NLT

Future Blessings

God has seasons in our lives. . . .
He is creating something you'll enjoy in the future.
You may not understand it today, but a month
or year later, you'll experience the benefits
of new growth He was watering.